The Old Testament: A Very Short Introduction

VERY SHORT INTRODUCTIONS are for anyone wanting a stimulating and accessible way in to a new subject. They are written by experts, and have been published in more than 25 languages worldwide.

The series began in 1995, and now represents a wide variety of topics in history, philosophy, religion, science, and the humanities. Over the next few years it will grow to a library of around 200 volumes — a Very Short Introduction to everything from ancient Egypt and Indian philosophy to conceptual art and cosmology.

Very Short Introductions available now:

Contents

The Old Testament

List of Illustrations

Chapter 1
What is the Old Testament?

Visitors to any of the great museums of the world will notice the contrast between the extensive displays of magnificent objects from ancient Egypt, ancient Syria, and ancient Mesopotamia, and those from ancient Israel, which are generally unimpressive and often difficult to find. Artistically, at least for museum curators, ancient Israel was a cultural backwater. Nothing from it is comparable to the tombs and temples of Egypt, the libraries and ziggurats of Babylon, or the glazed tiles and palaces of Persepolis.

Yet one artifact from ancient Israel has survived: its literature, commonly if somewhat controversially called the Old Testament. Prohibited according to an ancient law from making graven images, the Israelites channeled their creative energy into literary activity. Not that literature, even great literature, was exclusively an Israelite phenomenon in the ancient Near East—on the contrary, as we will see. But Israelite literature did not just survive; it became authoritative scripture in both Judaism and Christianity, and it has profoundly influenced and inspired believers, writers, artists, and musicians in the Western world and beyond.

In the literature of ancient Israel as preserved in the Old Testament, we encounter dozens of vividly drawn characters whose stories have been told over and over again, retelling that begins in the pages of the Bible itself. We are also introduced to concepts that have profoundly shaped religious beliefs, social values, and political institutions over the centuries, concepts such as covenant, commandments, chosen people, Promised Land, and divinely chosen rulers. Both the characters and the concepts occur in the context of a sweeping narrative of divine activity in history, from creation to the end of the first millennium BCE.

One understanding of the Old Testament is that it is an anthology of the literature of ancient Israel and early Judaism, comparable in scope to anthologies of English literature. Like such anthologies, it is a selection of works from more than a thousand years, and like them too it contains many kinds of writing—in the Old Testament there are myths, historical narratives, prophecies, fiction, laws, instructions for rituals, proverbs, and hymns, to name just some.

These kinds of writing are embedded in larger units called "books." For the most part each book is a relatively self-contained unit, but sometimes the separation between books is arbitrary. For example, the beginning of the book of Judges continues the narrative from the end of the book of Joshua without any break, and the same is true of the books of 1 and 2 Samuel, 2 Samuel and 1 Kings, and others. Within individual books, moreover, the genres are frequently mixed. The historical narratives in Genesis, for example, are sprinkled with both short and long poems, as well as with laws and accounts of rituals. Modern scholars have identified many more genres in Genesis, such as the novella in the Joseph story in chapters 37–50, myth in the first eleven chapters, genealogies, itineraries, lists, speeches, and so on. Thus, many of the books of the Old Testament, especially the longer ones, are also composites.

Modern scholars agree that the books of the Old Testament, and the parts that comprise them, were not written in the order in which they are now found but at various times over more than a thousand years. So, the Old Testament differs from standard anthologies of literature in an important way: the order of its first dozen or so books is based on the chronology of their narrative rather than on when they and their component parts were written. It is as if one were to start an anthology of English literature with *Paradise Lost*, because that epic, although written by Milton in the seventeenth century, describes events at the beginning of the world (at least as Milton believed it to have been), and then continue the anthology with the rest of English literature arranged by the times in which the works are set: ancient Greece, as in the nineteenth-century poet Tennyson's "Ulysses"; ancient Rome, as in Shakespeare's *Julius Caesar* from the late sixteenth century; ancient Britain, as in the Arthurian legends from various periods; the Middle Ages, as in the thirteenth-century poet Chaucer's *Canterbury Tales*; and the like.

The Old Testament follows a consecutive narrative chronology from Genesis through 2 Kings, from the creation of the world to the exile of Jews to Babylon in the sixth century BCE. After that, however, the narrative chronology is essentially abandoned, and books and parts of books move back and forth within and beyond

Older books

Occasionally the Old Testament refers to other books. Thus, in Numbers 21:14, an excerpt of poetry is identified as coming from "The Book of the Wars of the LORD." Another collection of ancient poems was "The Book of the Upright," quoted in Joshua 10:13 and 2 Samuel 1:18. Throughout the books of Kings and Chronicles there are repeated references to what seem to have been official royal records, including "The Book of the Acts of Solomon" and "The Book of the Kings of Judah and Israel." None of these ancient "books" has survived, but their mention shows that ancient Israelite literature was more extensive than that anthologized in the Old Testament.

that narrative framework. Some books of the Old Testament are arranged not chronologically but in descending order of length, as is also the case with other scriptures, such as the letters attributed to Paul in the New Testament and the suras in the Qur'an. At other times their arrangement seems arbitrary, as differences in order for many of them in the oldest complete manuscripts from late antiquity and the Middle Ages show. Different religious communities also present the books in different orders.

Different communities, different scriptures

A common explanation of the term Old Testament is that it is the first part of the Christian Bible. As usual in the study of religion, however, things are often more complicated than they first appear, and that definition needs to be clarified and even corrected.

Christianity began as one of several subsets of Judaism in the first century CE. It quickly moved away from its parent in beliefs and practices, in part because many non-Jews also became Christians. But as in parent-child relationships, the separation was never complete. Early Christian writers accepted the Jewish scriptures as authoritative—there was not yet a "New" Testament, for they were still writing it. Discussing "sacred writings," the second letter to Timothy describes them as "inspired by God and...useful for teaching, for reproof, for correction, and for training in righteousness" (2 Tim. 3:15–16). "Sacred writings" here means the Jewish scriptures, which at least since the early second century BCE had three parts: the Law, the Prophets, and the Writings. Under their Hebrew names, Torah, Neviim, and Ketuvim, these parts, abbreviated by the first letter of the names of each, eventually came to be called Tanak (also spelled Tanakh), a term Jews frequently use for the Bible.

The first part is the Torah, a word that means not only "law" but also "teaching" or "instruction." It consists of the first five books of the Bible, Genesis through Deuteronomy. Genesis opens with accounts of Creation and the Flood, and continues with stories of the ancestors of the ancient Israelites: Abraham and Sarah; Isaac and Rebekah; and Jacob and Leah, Rachel, Zilpah, and Bilhah and their children. The remaining four books, Exodus, Leviticus, Numbers, and Deuteronomy, continue the narrative of Genesis with the story of the Exodus, the escape of the descendants of Jacob from slavery in Egypt and their journey to the eastern border of the Promised Land. These four books cover a much shorter time than the many generations of Genesis. Their framework is the life of Moses, their principal human character: Moses's birth occurs in the second chapter of the book of Exodus, and his death and burial are described at the very end of Deuteronomy. Embedded in the narrative of these first five books of the Bible there are also hundreds of divinely given laws—hence the understanding of Torah as "law."

The second part of the Jewish scriptures is the Prophets, divided into the Former and Latter Prophets. The Former Prophets consists of the books of Joshua, Judges, Samuel, and Kings. These books continue the narrative where the Torah ended, relating the Israelites' history in the Promised Land of Canaan, from their conquest of that land under Moses's successor Joshua, through the often troubled history of the kings of Israel, and finally to the loss of the land to the Babylonians in the early sixth century BCE. The Latter Prophets are the books named after individual prophets. There are the three "major" prophets, so called because of their length: the books of Isaiah, Jeremiah, and Ezekiel, and the twelve "minor" or shorter prophets: the books of Hosea through Malachi.

The third part of the Jewish scriptures, the Writings, is a collection of works in several different genres, a kind of anthology within the larger anthology that is the Bible. There is poetry of various kinds in the books of Psalms, Proverbs, Song of Solomon, and Lamentations. There are reflections on the human condition in the book of Job, also mostly in poetry, and the book of Ecclesiastes.

There is historical fiction, as in the books of Ruth, Esther, and Daniel. The Writings also include historical narrative: the books of Chronicles cover the same chronological span as the Torah and Former Prophets, and conclude with the return from exile in Babylon in the second half of the sixth century BCE. The books of Ezra and Nehemiah continue this narrative, relating the history of the Jews in the late sixth and fifth centuries BCE.

By the end of the first century CE, these three parts—the Torah, the Prophets, and the Writings—had become the Bible of ancient Judaism, its "sacred scriptures," that is, writings believed to be divinely inspired and thus having a special authority. For Jews today, they are simply the Bible. Modern scholars often use the term Hebrew Bible to distinguish those books from the Christian Bible, which includes the New Testament as well, and also because the designation Old Testament, which was not used until the late second century CE, can be seen as pejorative, implying that the Jewish scriptures that comprise the "Old" Testament have apparently been superseded by the later writings that form the "New" Testament. But the term Hebrew Bible itself is something of a misnomer, since a few chapters of these scriptures are not in Hebrew, but rather in the closely related Semitic language of Aramaic.

Before the late first century CE various Jewish communities did not completely agree which books belonged to the category of sacred scripture. The Torah was fixed, as were the Prophets, but the Writings were more fluid. Other Jewish religious texts had been written toward the end of the biblical period and shortly thereafter, in the last two centuries BCE and the first century CE, and for some communities these writings were also scripture. One example is the book known as The Wisdom of Ben Sira (also called Sirach and Ecclesiasticus). Originally written in Hebrew around 200 BCE, this collection of proverbs and other poetry was translated into Greek in the late second century BCE by Ben Sira's grandson, who, by the way in his preface, mentions the division of scripture into

6

three parts, "the Law, the Prophecies, and the rest of the books." The Wisdom of Ben Sira was regarded by at least some Jewish communities as scripture and was revered well into the Middle Ages. For the most part, however, Jews have not considered it to be part of the Tanak.

Canons

Stabilizing the contents of the Bible in what came to be called a canon, an official list of the authoritative books, was a gradual process. By the end of the first century CE there was considerable agreement among various Jewish groups on which books were scriptural, but the status of some books continued to be debated. Although we have no explicit account of the process, several criteria seem to have informed it. One was that the book be in Hebrew (or Aramaic). Many of the books considered scripture by Jews in the Hellenistic world had been written in Greek, or, like the Wisdom of Ben Sira, were originally written in Hebrew but more widely circulated in Greek translations. A second criterion had to do with date: for a writing to be considered canonical, it should have been written no later than the mid-fifth century BCE, the time of Ezra, the last of the individuals thought to have been directly inspired by God. Jewish authorities therefore included in their canon works such as the book of Daniel; although modern scholars have concluded that it was written in the second century BCE, the book has as its hero—and for parts even its narrator—the character Daniel, who is described as living in the sixth century BCE. The same is true of other books that modern scholars date later than the time of Ezra. The book of Ecclesiastes, although probably written no earlier than the fourth century BCE, is attributed to Solomon, who was king of Israel in the tenth century BCE, and the book of Esther, probably to be dated to the fourth century as well, is set in the early fifth century. Books such as the Wisdom of Ben Sira, on the other hand, were clearly much later, as both their authorship and their content showed.

Many other factors were involved in defining the canon, but these two, language and antiquity, seem to have been paramount. So the books of Judith, Tobit, the Wisdom of Ben Sira, the Wisdom of Solomon, Baruch, and the books of the Maccabees, along with some additions to the books of Daniel and Esther, were in the end not included in the Tanak.

Before the process of canonization in Judaism was complete, however, Christianity had already begun to take shape, and very soon most Christians were Greek-speaking Jews and Gentiles. Early Christians, like some of their Jewish contemporaries in the Hellenistic world, accepted books such as the Wisdom of Ben Sira and Judith as scripture, and they were included in the Christian canon until the Reformation. It was then that Martin Luther (1483–1546), followed by other Reformers, decided that only the "Hebrew truth" should be part of the Christian Bible, and they limited their canon to those books found in the Tanak, the Hebrew Bible of Judaism. This conclusion was one that had earlier been implied by the great fifth-century CE Christian biblical scholar Jerome, who called these books Apocrypha, which literally means "hidden books" (although they were not really hidden), as opposed to the canonical books. Nevertheless, these books are still considered canonical by Roman Catholics and most Eastern Orthodox Christians; they are also called Deuterocanonical, in recognition of their somewhat ambiguous status.

The order of the books was another issue. The order of the books of the Torah was fixed by their narrative chronology, as were the Former Prophets. Until the Middle Ages, however, some Hebrew manuscripts included the book of Ruth among the Former Prophets, after the book of Judges, because it was set in the same period as that book. Eventually it was included among the Writings. The order of the books of the Latter Prophets also varied. Each of the longer books was apparently written on one scroll. In chronological order, the prophets for whom those books are named were Isaiah, Jeremiah, and Ezekiel, although again a different

1. A section of the book of Isaiah from one of the Dead Sea Scrolls, found in 1947. Dating to the second century BCE, it is the oldest complete manuscript of any book of the Bible. There are fifty-four columns on the parchment scroll; this one contains Isaiah 11:12–14.1. Each column is about ten inches high, and the entire scroll is about twenty-four feet long.

order was sometimes used. The Minor Prophets, Hosea through Malachi, also fit onto one scroll, and their order varied considerably. Within the Writings there was even more variation.

The early Christians believed that the Jewish scriptures in their entirety were a divinely revealed plan for the advent of Jesus, the Messiah—a plan, to be sure, that could not be deciphered until he had actually come. This was especially true of the Latter Prophets, and so from an early stage in Christian Bibles these books were placed last, immediately before the New Testament, which was seen as their fulfillment. That order is generally followed in modern Christian Bibles, although in many study Bibles the Apocrypha are inserted between the Prophets and the New Testament. There is a kind of theological logic in this rearranged order of the Jewish scriptures in Christian Bibles. The first part is a more or less continuous historical narrative dealing with the past—the books of Genesis through Esther (and, for some Christians, through the books of Maccabees). This sequence is followed by books that can be understood as dealing with the present: those concerned with the human condition, such as Job, Proverbs, and Ecclesiastes (along with the apocryphal Wisdom of Ben Sira and the Wisdom of Solomon), and the Song of Solomon, and with prayer, notably Psalms. Finally come the Prophets, thought to be about the future. Lamentations is included among the prophetical books, because the prophet Jeremiah was traditionally considered its author, as is the book of Daniel, probably because of the use of Daniel 7 by New Testament writers; in the Jewish canon both are grouped with the Writings.

The word *Bible* originally meant "book," but the Hebrew Bible or the Christian Old Testament is not one book but many, an anthology of ancient Israelite and early Jewish religious writings. Different religious communities have different versions of this anthology, as well as different names for it. Jews and Protestant Christians have the same contents, although in a different order. Roman Catholics and Orthodox Christians include in their Old Testament other authentic Jewish religious writings, the Apocrypha or the Deuterocanonical books. The result is a complicated listing. (For a chart of the various canons of Judaism and Christianity, see the appendix.)

The processes of canon formation also have a significant implication: Despite naïve views to the contrary, the Bible was not handed down by God as a complete package but was the result of a series of decisions made over the course of centuries by the leaders of different religious groups, decisions concerning a variety of works written by many authors also over the course of centuries.

Chapter 2
Interpretive strategies

Until the seventeenth century, the prevailing view of the Old
Testament among both Jews and Christians was relatively simple:
it was the word of God. Its human authors were in effect scribes
or secretaries, writing down what God dictated to them. In a
circular argument, this view was supported by the Bible itself.
Chapter after chapter of the books of Exodus, Leviticus, and
Numbers consist of direct divine speech to Moses, the leader of
the Exodus from Egypt, and speeches of prophets are repeatedly
introduced by the formula that "the word of the LORD came"
to them.

With the development of modern philosophy and modern science,
however, that prevailing view changed irrevocably, as previously
unquestioned dogmas were challenged from a variety of
perspectives. In the study of the Old Testament, the first issue
addressed was the authorship of the Torah, the first five books
of the Bible.

Moses and the Torah

According to early Jewish tradition, God had revealed the entire
contents of the Torah to Moses, who wrote it down. The ultimate
authority therefore was divine, and Moses was the supreme human
authority. That tradition was also accepted by the writers of the

New Testament, many of whom were Jewish themselves; when they quoted the Torah, they attributed it to Moses, as, according to them, Jesus did as well.

But did Moses really write the Torah? A few medieval scholars pointed out problems with this belief, such as the account at the end of Deuteronomy of Moses's death and burial. Moses, some proposed, could not have written that part of the Torah. But other scholars argued either that Moses, as a prophet, had had those events revealed to him, or that Moses's divinely designated successor Joshua had written those last few verses.

Not until the seventeenth century, with the beginning of modern philosophy, was the dominant view seriously questioned. Such thinkers as Thomas Hobbes, Baruch (Benedict) Spinoza, and Richard Simon began what the latter called "critical" scholarship. By critical Simon did not necessarily mean negative (although there are frequently negative aspects of biblical criticism), but rather without preconceptions derived from dogma.

Such freedom from presuppositions enabled thinkers to approach the Torah, and the Bible in general, as they would ordinary books and to consider issues such as style and consistency that inform our understanding of authorship.

One inconsistency that they noticed was the different names and titles used for God in the book of Genesis. According to Genesis 4:26, God had been called by the name *Yahweh* since the time of Adam, and it was as Yahweh that such people as Noah, Abraham, Isaac, and Jacob knew him. So, for example, when God speaks to Abraham he often refers to himself as Yahweh, and Abraham does the same. But according to Exodus 6:3, when Yahweh reveals his name to Moses, he says: "I appeared to Abraham, Isaac, and Jacob . . . , but by my name 'Yahweh' I did not make myself known to them." Clearly there is a contradiction here: either Abraham knew Yahweh by that name, or he did not.

The name of the God of Israel

Throughout the Old Testament, God is referred to by many names and titles. By far the most frequent, occurring nearly seven thousand times, is the sacred personal name of God, written in Hebrew with the consonants *yhwh*. Before the end of the biblical period this name came to be considered so holy that it was rarely spoken aloud, and so a word for "lord" (in Hebrew, *adonay*) was frequently used in its place. In translations of the Bible since antiquity this pious substitution has generally been followed; in modern English translations its presence is signaled by the use of small capitals: LORD is used whenever the text reads *yhwh*. Because *yhwh* was not pronounced, we are unsure exactly how it was vocalized, but the scholarly convention "Yahweh" is most likely correct.

Another issue concerned passages describing the same events, but with differing details. There are two accounts of the creation of the world and of humans at the beginning of the book of Genesis, two accounts of the Flood, several versions of the Ten Commandments, and so forth. Did God make animals before humans, as in Genesis 1:24–26, or did he first make a human, and then animals, as in Genesis 2:7, 19? Did God tell Noah to bring a pair of each species of animal into the ark, as in Genesis 6:19, or seven pairs of clean animals and only one pair of the unclean, as in Genesis 7:3? Did God give the Ten Commandments to Moses on Mount Sinai, as in Exodus 19:20, or on Mount Horeb, as in Deuteronomy 5:2? Such inconsistencies are hardly characteristic of great writers, whether divine or human.

There were other clear indications that Moses himself had not written the first five books of the Bible. When these books speak of him, it is always in the third person: the text tells what happened to Moses and is not Moses's own account of what he experienced. The text also frequently refers to times long after Moses, which would be anachronistic if Moses were the author. One example is the beginning of the book of Deuteronomy: "These are the words that Moses spoke to all Israel on the other side of the Jordan." Since Moses died east of the Jordan River valley, the narrative introduction must have been written not by Moses himself but by someone living west of the Jordan, after Moses's time.

The Documentary Hypothesis

From the late seventeenth to the late nineteenth centuries, these and other issues led scholars to conclude that the Torah, or as it is often called, the Pentateuch (from a Greek word meaning "five books"), is a composite. Beginning with the observation of different names and titles for God in the book of Genesis, scholars were able to isolate several distinct sources in the Pentateuch, each with its own characteristic vocabulary and themes. In its most fully developed form, this source analysis is called the Documentary Hypothesis, and it is the earliest important conclusion of modern critical scholarship.

The Documentary Hypothesis is, first of all, a hypothesis, a theoretical explanation of data. The data that it explains are the inconsistencies, the repetitions, the anachronisms, and other details that suggest not one but several different authors. In its classic formulation, these are explained by the existence of hypothetical documents or sources, written at different times by different authors and combined only at a relatively late date. In scholarly jargon, the identification and analysis of these sources in the text of the Pentateuch is often called literary criticism, an unfortunate term since it has little connection with the way most literature is interpreted; rather, it is source criticism. Although scholars have differed about how many sources there are, where they are found, and when they should be dated, in its most widely accepted form the Documentary Hypothesis states that behind the present text of the first five books of the Bible lie four earlier sources, commonly identified by letter. The earliest is the source called J (from the German spelling of the divine name, *Jahveh*, because many of the scholars who developed the hypothesis were Germans). In J, which was composed in the early first millennium BCE, God is called Yahweh from the beginning of the narrative (starting in Gen. 2:4), and he is a deity who often interacts personally and directly with humans. The next source is E, from a Hebrew word for "God," *Elohim*. It is a fragmentary source, dated slightly later than J. In E, God is called *Elohim* throughout Genesis, and his interactions with humans are less direct, often in dreams or through prophets or messengers rather than in person. The next source in chronological order is D, so called because it is almost entirely restricted to the book of Deuteronomy; it was written in the late eighth or seventh century BCE. The last of the four sources is P, for Priestly; compiled sometime in the mid-first millennium BCE, it focuses on matters of ritual and religious observance. In P, as in E, God is called *Elohim* throughout Genesis and until the revelation of the name Yahweh to Moses in Exodus 6. As the last of the sources, P is also the final editor of the Pentateuch, and thus the first chapter of the Torah, Genesis 1, and much of the last, Deuteronomy 34, are both from P.

Perceived as an attack on the doctrine that Moses had written the Torah, and implicitly on the authority of the Bible itself, the Documentary Hypothesis was repeatedly challenged, and many of its early proponents were condemned or forced to leave their teaching positions. By the end of the nineteenth century, however, it was widely accepted among Protestant scholars, although Jewish and Roman Catholic scholars did not join the consensus until the mid-twentieth century, and many conservative Jews and Christians still reject it.

By the late twentieth century the consensus appeared to be breaking up, as many scholars questioned the dates for the sources,

2. A silver amulet, now unrolled, found in a burial cave on the outskirts of Jerusalem. Written in the early sixth century BCE in ancient Hebrew, it contains a version of the Priestly Blessing found in Numbers 6:24–26: "May Yahweh bless and may he keep you; may Yahweh make his face shine upon you; and may he give you peace." It is the oldest surviving copy of a text occurring in the Bible.

The Documentary Hypothesis: an example

For the most part, the four sources occur in blocks of material that are juxtaposed. Occasionally, however, they are interwoven, as in the account of the plagues in Egypt (Exod. 7–11), and in the story of the Flood (Gen. 6–9), as the following excerpt from the latter illustrates. In this passage, according to the Documentary Hypothesis, there are only two sources, J (plain text), which uses "the LORD" (*yhwh*), and P (in italics), which uses "God" (*elohim*), and which have many other differences of detail.

> *Noah was six hundred years old when the flood of waters came on the earth.* And Noah with his sons and his wife and his sons' wives went into the ark to escape the waters of the flood. *Of clean animals, and of animals that are not clean, and of birds, and of everything that creeps on the ground, two and two, male and female, went into the ark with Noah, as God had commanded Noah.* And after seven days the waters of the flood came on the earth. *In the six hundredth year of Noah's life, in the second month, on the seventeenth day of the month, on that day all the fountains of the great deep burst forth, and the windows of the heavens were opened.* The rain fell on the earth forty days and forty nights. *On the very same day Noah with his sons, Shem and Ham and Japheth, and Noah's wife and the three wives of his sons entered the ark, they and every wild animal of every kind, and all domestic animals of every kind, and every creeping thing that creeps on the earth, and every bird of every kind—every bird, every winged creature. They went into the ark with Noah, two and two of all flesh in which there was the breath of life. And those that entered, male and female of all flesh, went in as God had commanded him;* and the LORD shut him in. (Gen. 7:6–16)

the very existence of some of them, and even the usefulness of source criticism for understanding the text as it now stands. Nevertheless, the Documentary Hypothesis is still a necessary starting point for interpreters, although most scholars would now agree that it alone does not fully explain the many processes that led to the final shape of the Pentateuch. Beginning in the early twentieth century additional methods of analysis were developed. One, known as *form criticism*, examines the smaller units that had been incorporated into the sources: identifying and understanding them makes it possible to think about the prehistory of the sources themselves. With the rise of disciplines such as anthropology and sociology, other methods also came to be used. Such development of interpretive strategies or methodologies has continued to the present, with a bewildering variety of criticisms and other "-isms" being used by biblical scholars: form criticism, redaction criticism, literary criticism (in the ordinary sense of that term), canonical criticism, structuralism, postmodernism, feminism, postcolonialism, and so forth.

Moses, authorship, and books

Let us return to the first question addressed by critical scholars: did Moses write the Torah? One could interpret the Bible as stating this. Several times in the books of Joshua and Kings "the book of the *torah* of Moses" or simply "the *torah* of Moses" is mentioned. But it is unlikely that this *torah* ("teaching" or "law") means the entire first five books of the Bible, since according to Joshua 8:32, Joshua was able to write it on stones. Nevertheless, that same verse also says that Moses himself had written that *torah*, and there are other references to Moses as a writer. For example, Exodus 24:4 states that "Moses wrote down all the words of the LORD," but in its context this must refer to the words that the Lord had spoken in Exodus 20–23, not the entire Pentateuch. Likewise, repeated references toward the end of Deuteronomy to the "book of the *torah*" that Moses wrote refer to the book of Deuteronomy itself, rather than to the preceding four books. The earliest mention of the "*torah* of Moses" (the "teaching" of Moses) that could mean the first five books of the Bible as such is in Ezra 7:6, which is set in the mid-fifth century BCE, long after the time when Moses might have lived.

Why then was Moses considered the human author of the first and most important part of the Old Testament? First, because he was the principal human character of the last four of the five books of the Torah. Second, throughout the ancient world it was commonplace to attribute one's own words to a distinguished authority from the past; examples of ancient notables who were given credit for words or compositions that they never said or wrote include David, Solomon, Socrates, and Jesus. In the period after the return from Babylon in the sixth and fifth centuries BCE, when the Jewish community was struggling with issues of belief and practice, the authority of Moses gave a special status to the first five books: they were the *torah*, the teaching of Moses himself.

There is another issue, having to do with ancient understanding of a book. In contrast to what we might have thought until recently, in antiquity a book was not necessarily a single product of a single author but was often more like a hypertext, which several, even many, writers might expand, edit, and otherwise modify. In this process, which went on for many generations, a variety of perspectives—or as the Documentary Hypothesis proposes for the Pentateuch, a variety of sources or traditions—were preserved. For its final editors, as for those of the entire Bible, preserving different sources was more important than superficial consistency of detail. Even before the Torah became sacred scripture, then, its constituent parts had already achieved something like canonical status. In the end, this process was endowed with the authority of Moses, the individual remembered as closer to God than anyone else in Israel's history.

Other challenges

The rise of modern philosophy, of critical thinking without presuppositions, or as Immanuel Kant put it in the late eighteenth century, awakening from dogmatic slumber, led to other important intellectual developments. Among these was the rise of modern science. A near contemporary of the seventeenth-century philosopher Spinoza, one of the first to challenge the doctrine that Moses was the human author of the first five books of the Bible, was Galileo Galilei, who along with Johannes Kepler adopted and elaborated the understanding of the solar system earlier proposed by Copernicus. The earth, Galileo and Kepler proved by scientific observation, orbited around the sun, not vice versa. This contradicted the view of the biblical writers and further challenged biblical accuracy, as would discoveries in geology and evolutionary biology in the nineteenth century. These scientific developments coincided with the formation of the Documentary Hypothesis, and for many believers both threatened the traditional authority of the Bible.

There was yet another source of information directly relevant to the Bible. Beginning in the mid-nineteenth century, early archaeologists of the Near East were discovering tens of thousands of texts, often written on clay tablets, from ancient Mesopotamia, which corresponds roughly to modern Iraq. Egyptian writing had been deciphered at the beginning of the century, and now the several scripts of the Sumerians, Babylonians, Assyrians, and other ancient Near Eastern peoples were also becoming available and were rapidly deciphered and read. These ancient texts were often directly pertinent to the Bible. Many contained myths, such as that of a great flood, which was parallel to the story of Noah in Genesis 6–9 in great detail. There were historical texts as well, mentioning many individuals and events previously known only from the Bible and providing independent confirmation of some details of biblical history—but by no means all of them.

Chapter 3
The Old Testament and history

The first dozen or so books of the Old Testament, depending on how one counts them and on the canon used, have a continuous narrative framework. They begin with creation and early human history in the opening chapters of Genesis. The rest of that book recounts the lives of four generations of Israel's ancestors, Abraham, Isaac, Jacob, and Jacob's twelve sons, the forefathers of the twelve tribes of Israel; by the end of Genesis Jacob and his extended family have migrated to Egypt. The four following books, Exodus, Leviticus, Numbers, and Deuteronomy, span a narrower period. They relate how under Moses's leadership the Israelites escaped from Egypt and journeyed to the eastern border of the Promised Land, where Moses died. Then we have a continuous history of the Israelites in the Promised Land: how they captured it under Joshua, in the book that bears his name; an account of their early days there, in the book of Judges; how they established a united monarchy under the first kings, Saul, David, and Solomon, in the books of Samuel and the first eleven chapters of 1 Kings. The rest of the books of Kings trace the history of the two kingdoms that separated after the death of Solomon: the Northern Kingdom of Israel and the Southern Kingdom of Judah. The Northern Kingdom comes to an end with its conquest by the Assyrians, and a little more than a century later the Babylonians conquer the Southern Kingdom.

Until the Enlightenment, this narrative framework was considered historical in the sense that it was accepted as an accurate, even inspired, account of what had taken place over thousands of years in the biblical writers' chronology. What the Bible said was true, in every detail.

That presupposition enabled James Ussher, archbishop of Armagh in Ireland in the seventeenth century, and other scholars to use figures given in the Bible to calculate that the creation of the world had occurred in 4004 BCE, that Abraham had lived from 1996 to 1821 BCE, and so on. The certainty with which such absolute dates were given was not entirely justified, because the numbers given both in the Bible itself and in the many different manuscripts of the Bible and its ancient translations were not always consistent, and other chronologies were also proposed. The primary method they used, however, was that of most historians from antiquity to the present: using dates known from a variety of ancient sources, such as the death of Alexander the Great in 323 BCE, and working back from them. But was the biblical record accurate when there was no corroboration?

By the late nineteenth century, developments in astronomy, geology, and other sciences, along with discoveries of ancient Near Eastern texts, had made it clear that in many details, and in terms of its chronology as well, the Bible was often unreliable and sometimes just wrong. Certainly the date for creation was no longer tenable, nor were dates for the many following generations in Genesis and subsequent books, in part because of the impossibly long life spans attributed to individuals, such as 969 years for Methuselah, 175 years for Abraham, and 120 years for Moses. The confidence that had made Ussher's chronology possible was irrevocably eroded.

Nonbiblical texts do provide some corroboration for the later periods of the history of ancient Israel. But the earlier one goes, the sparser the data are. For the period from Abraham to Moses, covered from Genesis 12 through the end of Deuteronomy, there are none; the same is true for the following period, from Joshua through the United Monarchy, the reigns of Saul, David, and Solomon. Only after the Northern Kingdom of Israel split from the Southern Kingdom of Judah is there independent confirmation of the biblical record. The first person in the Bible known from contemporaneous nonbiblical sources is the Egyptian pharaoh Shishak, mentioned in 1 Kings 11:40 and described as having attacked Judah in 1 Kings 14:25. Shishak, in Egyptian *Seshonq*, is well attested in Egyptian records, including one that recounts his campaign against Judah in about 925 BCE.

For the ninth century we have a few more correlations, and these increase significantly in the eighth century BCE and thereafter. Because of them the absolute chronology for the first half of the first millennium BCE is relatively firm, except for some minor inconsistencies between biblical and nonbiblical sources and among the latter as well.

Independent contemporaneous evidence is even more abundant for the sixth century BCE and later, as the Promised Land was ruled successively by the Babylonians, the Persians, the Greeks, and the Romans, for all of whom we have ample documentation. To be sure, these imperial powers usually had more important things on their minds than the tiny region of Judah, later to be called Judea, and their own records seldom refer to individuals or events there. But biblical sources repeatedly mention important foreign rulers, and from the mid-first millennium BCE onward the chronology is secure.

Inscriptions

Among the nonbiblical sources are ancient inscriptions from Israel and Judah. Hundreds of them dating to the first half of

Rulers of Israel and Judah

Israel (United Monarchy)

Saul (1025–1005)
  Ishbaal (1005–1003)
David (1005–965)
  Absalom (ca. 975?)
Solomon (965–928)

Southern Kingdom of Judah

Rehoboam (928–911)
Abijam (Abijah) (911–908)
Asa (908–867)

Jehoshaphat (870–846)

Jehoram (Joram) (851–843)
Ahaziah (Jehoahaz) (843–842)
Athaliah (842–836)
Jehoash (Joash) (836–798)

Amaziah (798–769)
Uzziah (Azariah) (785–733)
Jotham (759–743)

Ahaz (**Jehoahaz**) (735–715)

Hezekiah (715–687)
Manasseh (687–642)
Amon (641–640)
Josiah (640–609)
Jehoahaz (609)
Jehoiakim (608–598)
Jehoiachin (597)
Zedekiah (597–586)
  Babylonian conquest of the Southern Kingdom

Northern Kingdom of Israel

Jeroboam I (928–907)

Nadab (907–906)
Baasha (906–883)
Elah (883–882)
Zimri (882)
Omri (882–871)
Ahab (871–852)
Ahaziah (852–851)
Jehoram (851–842)

Jehu (842–814)

Jehoahaz (817–800)
Jehoash (**Joash**) (800–784)
Jeroboam II (788–747)
Zechariah (747)
Shallum (747)
Menahem (747–737)
Pekahiah (737–735)
Pekah (735–732)
Hoshea (732–722)
  Assyrian conquest of the Northern Kingdom

Notes: All dates are for years of rule, are BCE, and are approximate. Rulers mentioned in contemporaneous nonbiblical sources are in bold. Overlapping dates indicate coregencies.

the first millennium BCE have been excavated by archaeologists since the mid-nineteenth century. In recent decades, there has also been a flood of inscriptions purchased on the antiquities market, many of which are modern forgeries. Of the inscriptions that come from actual excavations, most are written on fragments of pottery, or potsherds. Their content, however, is often as fragmentary as the medium on which they are written. In addition, there is a handful of monumental inscriptions datable to the same period, and a similarly small number of papyri and writings in other media. There must have been many more texts that have not survived, probably because they were written on perishable organic materials such as papyrus. These inscriptions have some importance for understanding ancient Hebrew, but they rarely mention any individual or event known from the Bible, and so they are difficult both to date and to interpret.

The same is true of inscriptions from Israel's neighbors. From the first half of the first millennium BCE there are many texts from Aram (modern Syria), Phoenicia (modern Lebanon), and the kingdoms east of the Jordan Valley, Ammon, Moab, and Edom; again these rarely refer to important individuals or events known from other sources, including the Bible. One important exception is a monument from Moab known as the Mesha Stela.

Mesha, king of Moab, and his dealings with Israel

The Mesha Stela is a good example of the relationship between biblical and nonbiblical sources. Discovered in 1868 in the village of Diban, about thirty-five miles south of modern Amman, Jordan, and now in the Louvre in Paris, the Mesha Stela is a black basalt slab about 3.5 feet high. The text inscribed on it is in ancient Moabite, a language closely related to Hebrew, and describes in detail a Moabite victory over Israel under the leadership of King Mesha, who ruled in the mid-ninth century BCE.

This remarkable text corresponds in many ways with the book of Kings. Both mention the Moabite king Mesha, the Israelite king Omri, and Omri's successor, called Ahab in the Bible but not named in the Mesha Stela. Both refer to the national deities of Moab and Israel, Chemosh and Yahweh. Both understand military success or failure as the result of divine favor or punishment. And both refer to a common institution, the ban, in which a defeated population would be exterminated as a dedicatory offering to the deity of the victor.

The Mesha Stela recounts how Israel oppressed Moab during the reign of Omri, after which Mesha asserted his independence and captured Israelite territory. This is apparently summarized

Excerpt from the Mesha Stela

I am Mesha, the son of Chemosh-yat, the king of Moab, the Dibonite. My father ruled over Moab for thirty years, and I ruled after my father. And I made this high place in for Chemosh in Qarhoh . . . because he rescued me from all the kings and made me gloat over all my enemies.

When Omri was king of Israel, he oppressed Moab for many days because Chemosh was angry with his land. When his son succeeded him, he also said, "I too will oppress Moab in my days." That is what he said, but I gloated over him and his house, and Israel has perished forever. . . .

And Chemosh said to me, "Go, seize Nebo from Israel!" So I went by night and I fought with it from the break of dawn until noon, and I seized it and I killed all. . . . For I had put it to the ban for Ashtar-Chemosh. And I took from there the vessels of Yahweh, and I dragged them before Chemosh.

in 2 Kings 3:5, which tells us that "after the death of Ahab, Moab rebelled against Israel"; that rebellion is then described in greater detail and is set in the reign of Ahab's son and successor Jehoram. The biblical narrative recounts a victory over the Moabites by a coalition of the Northern Kingdom of Israel, the Southern Kingdom of Judah, and Edom, Moab's neighbor to the south. The victory was apparently not total, however, because Mesha was able to save one of his principal cities by sacrificing his son, and so, we are enigmatically told, "great wrath came upon Israel, so they withdrew" (2 Kings 3:27). The Mesha Stela apparently does not refer to the battle described in 2 Kings 3, and the biblical narrative makes no mention of the loss of Israelite lives and territory in Moabite territory. Perhaps both are partisan and partial accounts of separate episodes in an ongoing struggle between Moab and Israel.

The Mesha Stela and the book of Kings, therefore, are two independent sources that corroborate each other on basic information but do not tell exactly the same story. This is doubtless due to their respective political and religious perspectives, so both sources need to be interpreted.

Archaeology and the Bible

In addition to inscriptions, archaeologists also uncover another kind of evidence, called "material culture"—the walls, animal bones, pottery, tools, and other artifacts that have survived underground for thousands of years. Since the latter part of the nineteenth century archaeologists have excavated hundreds of ancient Israelite sites, many of which can be identified as places named in the Bible, including not only Jerusalem but also Megiddo, Jericho, Hazor, Lachish, and many others. As is the case with the Mesha Stela, however, the information unearthed at such sites is often difficult to synthesize with the biblical record, for two reasons. First, the biblical record itself is inconsistent, and also selective and ideological, not giving a comprehensive history of any single site but mentioning it when it suits the messages that the biblical writers are communicating. The second reason is the nature of archaeological evidence itself: material culture is mute. In only a handful of cases can we make a direct and unambiguous link between a person or event from the Bible and, say, a layer of ashes or the foundation of a city's wall. In the absence of anything like a "Kilroy [or Joshua, or David, or Omri] was here," dating the many aspects of material culture that have been excavated depends on a chain of inferences rather than on direct links and is frequently debated by specialists.

The important site of Megiddo provides an example. Strategically located at a major pass from the road along the Mediterranean coast to the hilly interior to the east, Megiddo was almost continuously occupied from the fourth millennium to the fourth century BCE. Excavations by German, American, and Israeli archaeologists in the twentieth century have uncovered some thirty strata or layers of successive settlements, with extensive fortifications, temples, palaces, water systems, and other remains; since the 1990s Megiddo has been the focus of a major joint Israeli–American expedition. Despite its obvious importance—it was one of the largest cities in ancient Israel—Megiddo is mentioned only a dozen times in the Bible and only sporadically in nonbiblical texts. The book of Joshua reports that the Israelites defeated the king of Megiddo, but that is contradicted by the book of Judges, which states that the Israelite tribe of Manasseh, in whose territory Megiddo was, did not succeed in driving out the city's Canaanite inhabitants; Judges also reports that Deborah led Israelite forces into battle against the Canaanites in the vicinity of Megiddo. Megiddo is further mentioned as the location of a major battle between the Egyptian pharaoh Neco and the Judean king Josiah in the late seventh century BCE (2 Kings 23:29).

3. The tell or mound of Megiddo, looking toward the northeast. It rises about one hundred feet above the plain and has an area of about seventeen acres on top.

The most discussed biblical reference to Megiddo is a cryptic statement in 1 Kings 9:15 that Megiddo was one of the cities whose walls King Solomon rebuilt. On the basis of this verse, the American excavators after World War I identified a wall and gateway as constructed during the Solomonic period (tenth century BCE), and also large structures inside the walls as stables, because a few verses later 1 Kings also mentions chariot cities, places where the chariot corps of the army was quartered. Megiddo, then, in a small way, apparently proved that the Bible was accurate. But subsequent excavations and more sophisticated dating techniques made it clear that neither the wall and gate nor the large buildings should be dated to the time of Solomon, but more likely to the time of the Israelite king Ahab a century later. Further, although Ahab is described in both biblical and nonbiblical sources as having had a large chariot force, it is far from certain that the large buildings were stables for chariot horses. Correlating the meager textual references with the extensive archaeological discoveries has been controversial, to say the least, and similar problems exist for almost every excavated site whose ancient identification is known.

As a result, it is now clear that archaeology cannot "prove" the Bible's historicity. What it does provide is the larger cultural context: the staging for the ongoing drama for which the Bible is the script.

History and earliest Israel

The evidence, then, is fragmentary, but when all of it is considered—texts from the ancient Near East, the Bible, and archaeological data—it does, generally, fit together. An analogy is a large jigsaw puzzle that is missing many of its pieces—but enough of them fit so that the reconstruction is probable, if not certain. This applies to chronology, and thus to persons or events, throughout the first millennium, that is, from the time of the division of the United Monarchy of Israel in the late tenth century to the time of the Maccabees in the second century BCE. With some diffidence we may push this back slightly, to David and Solomon, the second and third kings of Israel in the tenth century, but probably not before.

But what about earlier periods? Not a single person or event known from the books of Genesis through 2 Samuel is mentioned in a contemporaneous nonbiblical text. The only person named in the first five books of the Bible who also appears in relatively ancient nonbiblical sources is Balaam, the Mesopotamian prophet hired by the king of Moab to curse the Israelites on their journey from Egypt to the Promised Land, according to Numbers 22–24. He is the principal figure in an incomplete text written on plaster, from Deir Alla in the Jordan Valley, in which he is also identified as a seer. This extremely difficult text, however, dates from about 800 BCE and so is not contemporaneous with the narrative chronology of Numbers, although it does attest to Balaam's wide reputation.

We should also observe that the biblical sources for the earlier periods are remarkably unspecific. Although pharaohs of Egypt are described as having had dealings with biblical figures such as Abraham, Joseph, and Moses, none of the pharaohs referred to in the books of Genesis and Exodus is named by the biblical writers, so that we cannot fit them into the well-established chronology of ancient Egypt. Nor do Egyptian sources make any mention of the biblical figures. As a result, scholars have no conclusive answers to such questions as these: When did Abraham live or did he even exist? When did the Exodus from Egypt take place, if at all?

That is not to say that there may not be some authentic historical memory preserved in the narrative of earlier times, but it has been so refracted by the lenses of various sources that we can say little about what may actually have happened. The farther back we go in the biblical narrative, the more we are in the realm not of history but of myth.

Chapter 4
The Old Testament and myth

Among the countless ancient Near Eastern texts discovered, deciphered, and translated during the nineteenth and twentieth centuries, many thousands were identified as myths, and many more contained mythical elements. In its simplest sense, a myth is a narrative—the Greek word *mythos* originally meant story—in either prose or poetry, in which gods and goddesses are the principal characters. Although people sometimes find the idea shocking, the Old Testament is also imbued with myth.

Myths of origin

All religions seek to explain the unknown, and myths often provide such explanations. How did the world come to be? Why are we here? What will happen to us in the end? These and similar questions are the stuff of myths of origin, and such myths are widespread throughout the ancient Near East, with a bewildering variety of deities and explanations. Generally, the principal deity of a people, a nation, a city, or a region is described as the creator. Creation itself may be described as the result of a sexual act—for example, intercourse leads a goddess to give birth to the Euphrates River, or the land; a god masturbates and swallows his semen, becoming pregnant with his own offspring; or he swallows his father's testicles with the same effect. Such explicit sexuality in myth is not characteristic of the biblical accounts of Yahweh, although it may well have been present in popular Israelite religion.

A frequently occurring creation myth in the ancient Near East describes the creation of the world as the sequel to a titanic battle between the deity of the primeval chaotic waters and a storm god.

The Old Testament

The most elaborate description of a battle between cosmic forces that preceded creation is found in *Enuma Elish*. Also called *The Babylonian Creation Epic*, this is an ancient Mesopotamian hymn in praise of Marduk, the storm god and chief deity of Babylon. Here is an excerpt from its account of the combat between Marduk and Tiamat, the goddess of the primeval sea:

> Face to face they came, Tiamat and Marduk, sage of the gods.
> They engaged in combat, they closed for battle.
> The Lord spread his net and made it encircle her,
> To her face he dispatched the *imhullu*-wind, which had
>   been behind:
> Tiamat opened her mouth to swallow it,
> And he forced in the *imhullu*-wind so that she could not
>   close her lips.
> Fierce winds distended her belly;
> Her insides were constipated and she stretched her mouth
>   wide.
> He shot an arrow which pierced her belly,
> Split her down the middle and slit her heart,
> Vanquished her and extinguished her life.[1]

After the battle, Marduk formed the sky (the biblical "firmament" or "dome") from Tiamat's corpse, and he set into the sky the planets, moon, and constellations. Finally, with the help of the other gods, using the blood of one of Tiamat's divine allies, he created humans to serve the gods who had supported him.

In Mesopotamia the battle is between Tiamat, a goddess, and Marduk; in Canaan it is between Prince Sea and the god Baal. Elements of this widespread myth also pervade the Bible.

The most familiar account of creation in the Bible, that found at the beginning of Genesis, begins with an allusion to the battle before creation—darkness, as in a great storm cloud, is on the surface of the Deep, and God's wind is swooping over the water (Gen. 1:1-2)—but there is no description of the battle itself. Elsewhere in the Bible, however, the widespread myth of combat preceding creation occurs frequently.

Two passages from the Psalms illustrate biblical writers' familiarity with the mythical sequence of creation following a battle between the storm god and the sea:

You divided the sea by your might;
    you broke the heads of the dragons in the waters.
You crushed the heads of Leviathan;
    you gave him as food for the creatures of the wilderness.
You cut openings for springs and torrents;
    you dried up ever-flowing streams.
Yours is the day, yours also the night;
    you established the luminaries and the sun.
You have fixed all the bounds of the earth;
    you made summer and winter. (Ps. 74:13-17)

You rule the raging of the sea;
    when its waves rise, you still them.
You crushed Rahab like a carcass;
    you scattered your enemies with your mighty arm.
The heavens are yours, the earth also is yours;
    the world and all that is in it—you have founded them.
                                                (Ps. 89:9-11)

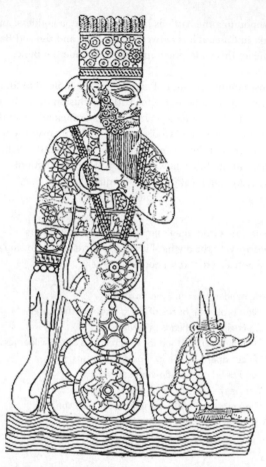

4. The Babylonian god Marduk, depicted on a ninth-century BCE cylinder, standing victorious on the sea dragon. In biblical tradition this dragon is called Leviathan, "the twisting serpent...in the sea" (Isa. 27:1).

In the Bible, the primeval sea has several names, some of which are the same as those used in nonbiblical texts, including Deep, Sea, River, Leviathan, and the dragon or the serpent. Others, such as Rahab, occur only in the Bible. Likewise, Yahweh the god of Israel is frequently described as a storm god. Like his Canaanite counterpart and sometimes rival Baal, he is the "rider on the clouds" (Ps. 68:4), whose voice is thunder (Ps. 29:3), and who reveals himself in a storm cloud (Nah. 1:3; Job 38:1).

As this summary discussion illustrates, in describing their patron god, the Israelites used the mythical vocabulary found throughout the ancient Near East. Their familiarity with myths is also evident in the account of the Flood in Genesis 6–9.

The Flood

The myth of a deluge caused by the gods is found in several different versions in Mesopotamian literature. These share with the biblical account of Noah and the Flood the rescue of a hero and his family in a boat built according to divinely given specifications, and the hero offering a sacrifice to the gods after the flood had subsided. An excerpt from the story of the flood in the epic of Gilgamesh provides an even closer parallel; the speaker is Utnapishtim, the hero of this Flood story, who is recounting what happened after his boat came to rest on a mountain:

> When the seventh day arrived,
> I put out and released a dove.
> The dove went; it came back,
> For no perching place was visible to it, and it turned round.
> I put out and released a swallow.
> The swallow went; it came back,
> For no perching place was visible to it, and it turned round.
> I put out, and released a raven.
> The raven went, and saw the waters receding.
> And it ate, preened, lifted its tail and did not turn round.

Then I put everything out to the four winds, and I made a
    sacrifice ...
The gods smelt the fragrance,
The gods smelt the pleasant fragrance,
The gods like flies gathered over the sacrifice.[2]

Likewise, in Genesis, after the Flood Noah released a raven once
and a dove three times, and offered a sacrifice to Yahweh, who
"smelled the pleasing odor" (Gen. 8:21). These and other close
correspondences make it clear that there is a connection between
the biblical and nonbiblical myths—if not a direct literary
dependence, then at least use of a common tradition.

Myth and history

Many historical texts have mythical components, as do
collections of laws and other genres as well. For example, in
the monument commemorating his victory over Israel in the
mid-ninth century BCE, the Moabite king Mesha reports how his
patron god Chemosh spoke to him and acted on his behalf.
Likewise, the Babylonian king Nebuchadrezzar (sometimes called
Nebuchadnezzar), who destroyed Jerusalem in 586 BCE, claims to
have been appointed shepherd over Babylon by the god Marduk,
just as his predecessor Hammurapi had more than a thousand
years earlier, at the beginning of his code of laws. Kingship, then,
although from our perspective a political institution, a form of
government, was, at least mythologically speaking, "lowered
from heaven"—established by the gods, who themselves had
chosen the king.

The same understanding is found in ancient Israel. Several kings of
Israel are described as having been personally chosen by Yahweh,
often through the mediation of prophets. King David was told by
Yahweh, "You shall be shepherd of my people Israel, you shall be
ruler over Israel" (2 Sam. 5:2), and, because Yahweh's reach was
eventually thought to include the whole world, using the same

language of the sixth-century BCE Persian king Cyrus, Yahweh says, "He is my shepherd, and he shall carry out all my purpose" (Isa. 44:28).

This use of mythological language to legitimate kingship was, one might argue cynically, a way to ensure the loyalty of those ruled: people would be less inclined to rebel against a divinely chosen ruler. Yet it also illustrates how in ancient societies the sacred and the secular were not nearly as distinct as we like to think they are in our own.

Myth and history, then, were not necessarily unrelated genres. History had a mythical dimension, and myth had a historical dimension. We can observe this in the first dozen books of the Bible. From the creation of the cosmos in Genesis 1 to the destruction of Jerusalem at the end of 2 Kings, the narrative has a continuous and often carefully calibrated chronology, moving without a break from the mythical material in the early chapters of Genesis to the stories of Israel's ancestors, and then on to the Israelites' escape from Egypt, their entry into the Promised Land, and their history there. The primary actor in this continuous narrative is Yahweh, and that gives it a mythical dimension, at least in terms of the basic meaning of myth as a narrative in which a divine being is the principal character.

Yet despite this mythical component, and despite the complex prehistory of the narrative, it also obviously has a historical component. The books of Kings meticulously trace the parallel histories of the kings of Israel and Judah from the late tenth to the sixth centuries BCE, and refer often to events on a larger stage—in Egypt, in Syria, in Mesopotamia. While aware of the political, military, economic, natural, and other forces that shaped their history, most biblical writers, like their contemporaries, also viewed that history on a higher level as the continuing interaction of their god with human beings. For the biblical historians and prophets, the successes and failures of the Israelites were ultimately interpreted as divinely bestowed rewards or, more frequently, punishments.

God and the gods

The biblical writers knew that most peoples worshipped gods other than Yahweh, and they frequently mention deities such as the Egyptian god Amun; the Babylonian gods Marduk (also called Bel and Nebo) and Nergal; Canaanite deities, including the grain god Dagon, the storm god Baal, the plague god Resheph, the god of death Mot, and the goddesses Asherah and Astarte, as well as the national gods Chemosh of Moab, Milcom of Ammon, and Hadad of Aram.

The Bible also reports frequently that the Israelites worshipped the same gods that their neighbors did. In Egypt, before the Exodus, they served other gods (Josh. 24:14; Ezek. 20:5–8), and they continued to do so once they entered the Promised Land. King Solomon reportedly worshipped Astarte, Milcom, and Chemosh (1 Kings 11:5–7). Biblical historians and the prophets repeatedly condemn the Israelites for their failure to worship only Yahweh. They also worshipped Baal and Astarte (Judg. 2:13), Tammuz, a dying and rising god of Mesopotamia (Ezek. 8:14), the sun (Ezek. 8:16; see also 2 Kings 23:11), and the queen of heaven (Jer. 44:17), as well as such malevolent forces as Azazel (Lev. 16:8) and Lilith (Isa. 34:14). Ancient Hebrew inscriptions also provide evidence for the worship of other gods, as do personal names such as Jerubbaal, Ishbaal, Meribbaal, and Baalyada (or Beeliada), all of which contain the divine name Baal.

But it was not only unenlightened foreigners and unfaithful Israelites who believed in other gods. Throughout the Old Testament other gods are associated with Yahweh. Like a human king, and like other ancient Near Eastern gods, Yahweh presided over a kind of royal court, with ministers and attendants. The members of this heavenly court included a large number of deities, who were Yahweh's heavenly army or "host"—he is the "god of hosts." Among them were cherubim (sphinx-like composites) and seraphim (probably winged serpents, as in Egyptian religion); messengers, later identified as angels (the English word "angel" is derived from the Greek word *angelos,* which means "messenger"); and the heavenly bodies. Collectively, this pantheon was known as the "sons of God," and they functioned as Yahweh's council, advising him and also singing his praises. So Yahweh is the "most high," but he is not alone; rather he is the head of an assembly of gods, who are his "holy ones."

The many references to other gods as Yahweh's retinue raise the question of what the biblical writers actually believed. Did they think of Yahweh as one among many gods, even if he was the

One of the most explicit examples of mythology in the Bible is Genesis 6:1–4.

> When humans began to multiply on the face of the ground, and daughters were born to them, then the sons of God saw how beautiful the human daughters were, and they took wives for themselves from any that they chose. Then Yahweh said, "My breath shall not remain in humans forever, for they are flesh; their days shall be one hundred twenty years." The Nephilim were on the earth in those days—and also afterward—when the sons of God went in to the human daughters, who bore children to them: these were the warriors of old, the men of renown.

As in other ancient myths, divine beings are described as marrying human women and producing a generation of heroes. No other details are given in this short passage, which must be a fragment or summary of a fuller mythical tradition.

highest of them? Or is this use of mythology more literary in nature, as when Milton in *Paradise Lost* invokes the Muse in imitation of classical epics? Or is it just an unexamined archaism, as when we say that the sun rises and sets even though we know better? When we take into account the many similarities between the descriptions of Yahweh and those of other deities in the ancient Near East, along with the many references to Israelites worshipping other gods in the Bible, it is probable that the biblical writers at least in earlier periods were not monotheists in the strictest sense—that is, they did not categorically deny the existence of other gods but regarded them as subordinate to Yahweh. Because Yahweh was "a jealous god" (Exod. 20:5), only he was to be worshipped, as the first commandment states: "You shall have no other gods before me" (Exod. 20:4–5).

By the late biblical period a strict monotheism had developed, and these references to other gods were then not understood literally. Monotheism created its own problems, however: how to deal with the polytheism of the earlier writings, and how to explain the presence of evil and suffering in the world.

Chapter 5

The Exodus from Egypt: a deep probe

The typical Near Eastern archaeological site is called a tell, an artificial mound created by successive layers of human occupation over centuries and often millennia. When archaeologists excavate a tell they cannot possibly expose all of the layers in their entirety from the most recent to the earliest. Instead, in order to uncover part of the earlier settlements, they sink deep probes or soundings through the various layers down to bedrock. In some ways the Old Testament is like a tell, with layers of material superimposed by various generations throughout the history of ancient Israel. In this chapter we will sink a probe into one section, chapters 1 through 15 of the book of Exodus.

These chapters are part of a continuing narrative, the story of the "sons of Israel," that is, the descendants of Jacob, whose name had been changed to Israel in Genesis 32:28. Because of a famine in the land of Canaan, this group moved to Egypt, where they suffered persecution and even attempts at extermination, but God intervened to save them, and under the leadership of Moses they escaped from Egypt. Within this narrative framework, however, is a veritable jumble of material, full of inconsistencies and a bewildering variety of sources and genres.

Source analysis

In Exodus 1–15, as in the books of Genesis and Numbers, we encounter three of the four principal sources of the Documentary Hypothesis, Yahwist (J), Elohist (E), and Priestly (P). Each has its own characteristic vocabulary and themes. Thus, the mountain where God appears to Moses in the burning bush, and later reveals the Ten Commandments and other laws to him, is called Horeb in E (Exod. 3:1), the same name used in Deuteronomy, although both J and P will call it Sinai (beginning in Exod. 19). In J, Moses's father-in-law is Reuel (Exod. 2:18), whereas a few verses later, E names him Jethro (3:1). In J, Moses is the primary human actor, whereas in E Moses and Aaron are almost equal, and in P Aaron gets star billing. And, in a passage that exhibits both the repetition that has resulted from the combination of the sources and the different names used for the deity, in Exodus 3:7–8, which are J, Yahweh is referred to by that name, but in the very similar following verses (3:9–12), which are E, he is called God (*elohim*). Not until Exodus 3:15 in E, and 6:2 in P, will God reveal his personal name, Yahweh, to Moses, and after that all sources generally use it.

In part at least because originally independent sources have been combined, there are inconsistencies throughout the narrative. If Moses's escape from Pharaoh's decree that all male infants should be killed was exceptional, then how did Aaron survive, to say nothing of the six hundred thousand men who reportedly left Egypt (Exod. 12:37)? If there were six hundred thousand men, then the number of women must have been approximately the same—but how could two midwives (1:15) have served such a large population? If Moses was raised by Pharaoh's daughter (2:10), then why did he imply that he had no standing in the Egyptian court (3:11)? Did Yahweh reveal his name to Moses in Midian, as E has it (3:1), or after he had returned to Egypt, as in P's account (6:1–2)? Source analysis explains *why* such inconsistencies exist, but not where they came from.

Form criticism

Behind the sources lie many forms or genres. There are itineraries, rituals, laws, genealogies, folktales, hymns, and theophanies, all incorporated into the continuous narrative but often showing signs of their originally independent origins.

As an example let's take a look at this short passage in Exodus 4:24–26:

> On the way, at a place where they spent the night, Yahweh met him [Moses] and tried to kill him. But Zipporah took a flint and cut off her son's foreskin, and touched Moses's feet with it, and said, "Truly you are a bridegroom of blood to me!" So he let him alone. It was then she said, "A bridegroom of blood by circumcision."

In this enigmatic snippet, which belongs to the J source, we encounter an unpredictable and dangerous deity attempting to kill Moses as he is on his way back to Egypt to carry out his mission to tell Pharaoh to let Yahweh's people go. As in Genesis 32:22–32, the deity is presented as a kind of night demon—as Hosea puts it, "a lion, a leopard lurking beside the way" (Hos. 13:7).

In its final form, the episode serves as an implicit etiology—a narrative explanation of a phrase well known to its ancient audiences but not entirely clear to us, in this case "bridegroom of blood." The phrase is linked by the narrative with circumcision, probably because that procedure was originally, and appropriately, a ritual having to do with marriage and reproduction, rather than one performed at birth as Genesis 17 presents it. In any case, Moses's unnamed son has not been circumcised, nor, apparently, has Moses, which may be why Yahweh wants to kill him. But Zipporah, Moses's wife, acts quickly to avert disaster: she circumcises her son, and then touches the bloody skin to Moses's genitals (for which "feet" is a frequent biblical euphemism), tricking Yahweh into thinking that Moses too has been circumcised.

Etiologies are one of the principal genres throughout the first several books of the Bible, serving to link the narrative of the distant past with the rituals, customs, names, features of the landscape, ancestry, and other circumstances familiar to the audiences for whom the narrative was written. Thus, Moses's name is explained by a pun because although it is technically Egyptian, as in the name of the Pharaoh Thutmoses, it sounds like a rare Hebrew word that means "to draw out [of water]" (Exod. 2:10). Similarly, the origin of the festival of Passover is explained by the Israelites' escape from the final plague, the killing of the firstborn, when Yahweh "passed over" their houses (Exod. 12:26–27), and the name Marah, the place where the Israelites first stopped in the desert to the east of Egypt, is explained by the bitterness (Hebrew *mar*) of the water there (15:23).

Other analyses

Zipporah, a woman, is also a circumciser. That in itself is remarkable, as feminist scholars have pointed out. Moreover, her decisive action is reminiscent of those of other women in the narrative, including the midwives Shiphrah and Puah, who thwart Pharaoh's decree to kill all the newborn males; Moses's mother and sister, who arrange his rescue; and even Pharaoh's daughter, who adopts him. We should also note that Miriam, curiously identified as Aaron's sister but not Moses's (but see Num. 26:59), and also as a prophet, leads a victory song (Exod. 15:20–21). The words that she and the other women chant—"Sing to Yahweh, for he has triumphed gloriously; horse and rider he has thrown into the sea" are the opening of the longer song earlier attributed to Moses and the Israelites (Exod. 15:1); could it be that Miriam was the author of the entire song, but that it was later attributed to Moses? Feminist scholars have appropriately pointed to these passages as an important counter to the prevailing patriarchalism of the Bible and of its interpretation.

Another type of analysis, sometimes called canonical because it treats the Bible in its final form rather than just exploring the history of its formation, connects the brief episode of the circumcision with the final plague in Exodus 11–12. In that event Yahweh is again a deity who kills at night, and again death is averted by a sign of blood, this time that of a lamb. Another example of this kind of canonical or contextual analysis on an even larger scale connects Moses with Noah. The Hebrew word for the boat that Moses's mother makes for him is the same word used for Noah's ark in Genesis 6–8, and these are the only two places where the word in used in the Bible. Like Noah's ark, Moses's boat is waterproofed (Gen. 6:14; Exod. 2:3, although different words are used). The narrator thus links Noah, who saved the human species from the waters of the Flood, with Moses, the human savior of the Israelites, whose survival in water anticipates the event at the sea that occurs in Exodus 14.

The narrative and history

As with the preceding book of Genesis, and as will continue to be the case until well into 1 Kings, there is no direct link between the persons and events described in Exodus 1–15 and nonbiblical sources. In the abundant texts from ancient Egypt, there is no mention of Moses or Aaron, nor of plagues, nor a killing of the firstborn, nor the drowning of Pharaoh's army. Now absence of evidence is not, as Carl Sagan put it, evidence of absence, and it is at least possible that, as is often true of the ancient Egyptians and other powers throughout history, defeats were simply not recorded. But there is no evidence.

The biblical account in Exodus is also tantalizingly vague. Who was the Pharaoh who began the persecution of the Hebrews, as the Israelites are often called in these chapters? Who was his successor, with whom Moses and Aaron had dealings? Both are unnamed. If the biblical writers had identified one of these pharaohs, we would know at least when they thought the events they narrate occurred. But they do not, and so, even if we presume that there is a historical kernel to the events, we cannot date them with certainty.

Two principal dates for the Exodus have been proposed. The earlier, in the sixteenth century BCE, has been suggested since antiquity, connecting the Exodus with the expulsion from Egypt of dynasties of non-Egyptian origin known as the Hyksos. But there are problems with this, including the lack of references to Egypt as a political power in the succeeding books of Joshua and Judges, which according to this date would be set in a period when Egypt exercised direct control over the land of Canaan. A majority of modern scholars, although by no means all, prefer a date in the mid-thirteenth century BCE, during the long reign of the Pharaoh Rameses II (1279–1213). This is at best an educated guess, based on parallel lines of evidence that do not intersect.

Nor is the geography clear. Few of the many places named in Exodus 1–15 can be identified with any probability. It is likely, although by no means certain, that the cities Pithom and Rameses reportedly had built by the Hebrew slaves (Exod. 1:11) are the modern sites of Tell er-Retabah and Tell ed-Dab'a in the eastern Nile Delta, the same region where both Genesis and Exodus place the Hebrews. The body of water that the Israelites crossed safely and in which, according to some accounts, the Egyptians were drowned, is traditionally translated "Red Sea." The Hebrew term here (*yam suf*) can be used for the western arm of that sea, the Gulf of Aqaba or Eilat (1 Kings 9:26). But *yam suf* literally means "sea of reeds," and so many scholars identify it not as the Red Sea but as one of several smaller shallow lakes or wetlands between the Nile Delta and the northern Sinai Peninsula. This view is supported by a somewhat prosaic tradition of the event at the sea, in which the escaping slaves, on foot, were pursued by the Egyptians, in chariots, but the chariots got stuck in the mud (Exod. 14:24–25).

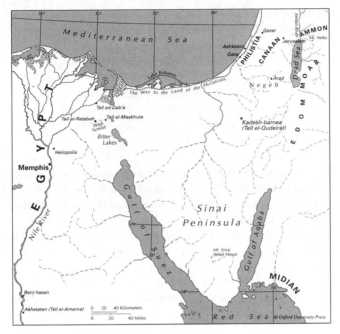

5. The geography of the Exodus from Egypt.

The narrative and myth

Scholars have often identified various plagues, such as hail, locusts, and cattle plague, as natural occurrences. But the point of the narrative is that they are not natural but supernatural, that is, caused by Yahweh. This is evident, for example, in the restriction of the plagues of cattle disease, hail, and darkness to the Egyptians, with the Israelites unaffected (Exod. 9:6, 25–27; 10:23). In other words, these are mythical events.

The mythical dimension of the narrative is evident not just in many details but also in its overarching plot, in which Yahweh's direct intervention controls events. The contest between Moses (and Aaron) and Pharaoh (and his magicians) is also a contest between Yahweh and the Egyptian deities, a contest in which Yahweh ultimately defeats them, as he predicts: "I will pass judgment on all the gods of Egypt" (Exod. 12:12)—so it seems that Yahweh is not (yet) a monotheist himself! Thus, after the escape, the hymn asks the rhetorical question "Who is like you, O Yahweh, among the gods?" (Exod. 15:11)—Yahweh has proven his superiority to all other deities.

The account of the event at the Sea of Reeds makes use of the widespread tradition of the defeat of the primeval sea by the storm god. Yahweh the storm god blows with his wind, through his nostrils (Exod. 15:8, 10), and defeats his enemy. But in the Exodus use of the myth, the enemy is not the chaotic primeval sea but Pharaoh and his army, and the sea is an instrument in that victory. Still, there are allusions to the earlier myth: as in the battle before creation, the divine wind blows the sea back, and the dry land appears as the waters are divided (Exod. 14:21; compare Gen. 1:2, 9).

In other biblical accounts of the Exodus, the mythology is explicit. Thus, a poetic summary of the event relates that "when Israel went from Egypt . . . the sea looked and fled . . . at the presence of the Lord" (Ps. 114:1, 3, 7), just as in the ancient combat myth the primeval waters cowered before the storm god. Similar language is used in Psalm 77:

> When the waters saw you, O God,
>> when the waters saw you, they writhed;
>> the very deep trembled.
> The clouds poured out water;
>> the skies thundered;
>> your arrows went everywhere.
> The crash of your thunder was in the whirlwind;
>> your lightnings lit up the world;

the earth trembled and shook.
Your way was through the sea,
your path, through the mighty waters;
yet your footprints were unseen.
You led your people like a flock
by the hand of Moses and Aaron. (Ps. 77:16–20)

Still later, an anonymous sixth-century BCE prophet explicitly
connected the primeval combat with the Exodus, moving
seamlessly from the defeat of the sea dragon, here called Rahab, to
the Exodus:

Was it not you who cut Rahab in pieces,
who pierced the dragon?
Was it not you who dried up the sea,
the waters of great Deep;
who made the depths of the sea a way
for the ransomed to cross over? (Isa. 51:9–10)

The Exodus in biblical tradition

Because of both the lack of any historical evidence and the use of
mythological language, it is impossible to say what actually
happened. Was there one Exodus, or several? Was it a relatively
small group of slaves who managed to escape, or several million?
Did the event (or events) take place in the mid-second millennium,
or later? We cannot answer these questions.

Yet the Exodus pervades biblical tradition. It is the paradigmatic
event—the crossing of the Jordan River as the Israelites entered
the Promised Land is explicitly linked to the crossing of the Sea of
Reeds (Josh. 4:23), and, much later, the return from exile in
Babylon in the sixth century BCE will be understood as a new
Exodus (Isa. 43:15–21). Moreover, the Passover, one of ancient
Israel's—and subsequently, Judaism's—primary religious
observances, although originally a composite agricultural festival,

was from an early stage understood as a reenactment and commemoration of the Exodus.

Given its thematic presence throughout the Bible, the Exodus is unlikely to be just fictional. Rather, embedded in the many literary and mythological embellishments is an authentic historical memory of an event that the participants, probably a small group of runaway slaves, identified as the decisive action of their god on their behalf. That event, celebrated in song, in ritual, and in narrative, gave them an identity that against all odds they have maintained to this day. It was a formative event, making them who they were—the people Yahweh had chosen as his "treasured possession" (Exod. 19:3).

Because of the importance of the Exodus, laws, rituals, institutions, and other aspects of Israelite society were linked to it. To take just one example, the Ten Commandments are viewed as their response to what Yahweh had done for them: "I am Yahweh your God, who brought you out of the land of Egypt, out of the house of slavery" (Exod. 20:1).

This probe into Exodus 1–15 illustrates the complexity of biblical traditions. Almost every biblical text is composite in the sense that unlike modern works it was not written once and then considered complete; rather, a text was subject to constant modification, variation, commentary, elaboration, expansion, and other types of addition and editing as writers from later generations continued to add their insights.

At the same time, the Exodus narrative also illustrates the intersection of history and myth. For the biblical writers, Yahweh was the primary actor in history—as modern scholars have put it, he was the "lord of history," although that is not a biblical phrase. Whatever happened was ultimately Yahweh's doing; the challenge was to fathom exactly what he was doing and why. Or, as we have put it more academically above, history had a mythical dimension.

Chapter 6
"Keep my commandments": biblical law

According to the book of Exodus, following their escape from Egypt the Israelites headed toward Mount Sinai, where they arrived after a two-month journey. There Yahweh appeared to them with all the manifestations of the storm god—"thunder and lightning, as well as a thick cloud" (Exod. 19:16), and in a series of speeches to Moses gave the Israelites their laws. One of the meanings of the word *torah* is "law," and much of the Torah, the first five books of the Bible, consists of divinely given laws— according to early Jewish scholars, 613 in all.

Most of these laws are found in three major collections. They are often called codes, as are other ancient Near Eastern legal collections, of which a dozen are known. But that term is somewhat misleading, since these collections are not comprehensive, like the Code of Justinian or the Napoleonic Code, nor are they cited in records of judicial proceedings. Yet the general ethic of the biblical collections is often found in other parts of the Bible, such as the prophets and the book of Proverbs, and so it is likely that the collections reflect actual legal practice.

The three principal collections are the Covenant Code in Exodus 20:22—23:19, the Holiness Code in Leviticus 17–26, and the Deuteronomic Code in Deuteronomy 12–24. Although the first

6. The upper part of the stela that contains the Code of Hammurapi, the most well-known ancient nonbiblical collection of laws, dating to the eighteenth century BCE and found in Susa, in modern Iran, in 1900. The sun god Shamash, on the right, is shown giving to King Hammurapi insignia of royal power. In the text immediately beneath the image, Hammurapi tells how the gods had made him king "to make justice prevail in the land . . . to prevent the strong from oppressing the weak."

and the third especially overlap considerably, there are also many differences of detail. On the basis of these similarities and differences we can reasonably conclude that there was a consistent legal tradition in ancient Israel, but with both regional and chronological variants.

The Covenant Code

Laws are windows into a society—its principles of organization, its values, and its ideals. Let us examine the Covenant Code as a sample of ancient Israelite law. It is probably the oldest of the several biblical legal collections, dating perhaps as early as the end of the second millennium BCE. It contains laws dealing with marriage, property, slavery, theft, assault, loans, perjury, various forms of homicide, and criminal negligence. Interspersed with these civil and criminal matters are also religious obligations and prohibitions. The laws are formulated in two distinct ways. Some

An example of case law

If a man allows a field or vineyard to be grazed over, or lets livestock loose to graze in someone else's field, he shall make restitution from the best of his field or the best of his vineyard. If fire breaks out and catches in thorns so that stacked grain or standing grain or [grain growing in] the field is consumed, the one who started the fire shall make full restitution. (Exod. 22:5–6)

There are other ways that a neighbor's field could be damaged or his crop ruined, possibilities that this case-specific law does not include; perhaps it deals only with the most frequent, while establishing the general principle that restitution is to be made for culpable negligence.

are case-specific, beginning with a conditional clause: "If [*or* when]...then..." Others are more absolute, like the Ten Commandments, giving a general command or prohibition and often beginning with "Whoever...." or "You shall (not)..."

The society that these laws depict is primarily a rural, agricultural one, where the inhabitants live in houses, presumably clustered in villages or towns. The crops grown include grain, grapes, and olives, and the domesticated animals mentioned are oxen, donkeys, sheep, goats, and dogs. It is thus the typical Mediterranean economy—ancient and modern—but not really appropriate for a group of runaway slaves camped at the base of a mountain in the semi-arid wilderness of the Sinai Peninsula. These laws must come from a later period when the Israelites were already settled in the Promised Land, and like much other material that the narrative connects with the revelations at Mount Sinai, the collections of laws have been anachronistically inserted into that context.

In the society presupposed by the laws of the Covenant Code there is apparently no centralized political organization, in contrast to the later Deuteronomic Code, which refers to the king (Deut. 17:14–20). Judicial procedures were probably handled at a local

Examples of general law

Whoever strikes his father or his mother shall be put to death.
Whoever kidnaps a man, whether he has been sold or is still held in possession, shall be put to death.
Whoever curses his father or his mother shall be put to death.
(Exod. 21:15–17)
You shall not allow a female sorcerer to live. (22:18)
You shall not boil a kid in its mother's milk. (23:19)

level, although there are no unambiguous references to actual judges in the original Hebrew of the Covenant Code. The Deuteronomic Code is more explicit; in it, even though there was some centralized government, many cases were still resolved locally, as Deuteronomy 16:18 makes clear: "You shall appoint judges and officials throughout your tribes, in all your gates ... and they shall render just decision for the people."

Some cases, however, could not be resolved—as when there was conflicting testimony with no evidence to support one side over the other. In such cases, appeal was made to local religious authorities, who used other means to reach a decision.

Values

The laws of the Covenant Code depict a stratified society. Men— fathers and husbands—were the heads of the family, with absolute authority over their households. They controlled women, especially daughters, who could be sold as slaves, and whose value was dependent upon their virginity: if an unmarried daughter was seduced, then the seducer had to make restitution to her father for what was essentially her diminished value.

It was also a society in which slavery was an accepted institution. There were strict laws concerning the treatment of slaves—some fairly arbitrary, such as that punishing an owner whose slave dies immediately after a beating but not one whose slave dies a day or two later (Exod. 21:20–21); some even cruel, such as the requirement that a slave's wife and children acquired during a limited term of slavery (probably as a way of paying off a debt) belonged to the owner when the slave was set free, or, if the slave was unwilling to leave his family behind, he could agree to become a slave for life (21:2–6); and some from our perspective relatively enlightened—given the very existence of slavery—such as the emancipation of a slave who had been abused by his owner (21:26–27).

In this society, primary horizontal relationships concerned the neighbor (Exod. 21:14; 22:7–8, 10–14, 26–27). As the Holiness Code puts it, "You should love your neighbor as yourself" (Lev. 19:18). In the Israelite legal system a neighbor was a fellow Israelite, not necessarily one living nearby. Distinguished from the neighbor was the stranger or (resident) alien, not a full member of the community but one who nevertheless also had rights, including that of rest on the Sabbath. In the laws concerning aliens (and concerning slaves in other collections), repeated reference is made to the Israelites' experience in Egypt: "You shall not oppress a resident alien; you know the soul of an alien, for you were aliens in the land of Egypt" (Exod. 23:9). The implicit principle here is that of imitation of God: the Israelites are to remember their experience in Egypt and not only have empathy for those in similar situations but also to treat them as God had treated the Israelites. So, the Holiness Code also commands, "You shall love the alien as yourself" (Lev. 19:34).

The prophets emphasize this obligation to less powerful members of society: the resident alien, the poor, and those without a male protector, the widow and the fatherless—the usual translation "orphan" obscures the patriarchal social structure: in biblical law an orphan is technically a child without a male parent.

A possible offset to the prevailing patriarchy is the status of the mother, as the mention of "father and mother" (in Exod. 21:15, 17) implies. In this patriarchal milieu we would not be surprised if the text simply said, "Whoever strikes his father shall be put to death," but it includes the mother as well. A parallel law in the Code of Hammurapi offers an interesting contrast: "If a son should strike his father, they shall cut off his hand."[1] Here only the father is mentioned, not the mother—but the penalty is less severe!

After the laws have been given, the Israelites ratify the "book of the covenant" (Exod. 24:7—hence the designation Covenant Code), and their acceptance of its terms is solemnized with a blood ritual. But what precisely is a covenant?

Covenant and Decalogue

Covenant is one of the central themes of biblical tradition, so important that it gives its name to the two parts of the Bible in the Christian canon, the "Old Covenant" (for that is what "testament" means), and the New. The Hebrew word for covenant, *berit*, occurs nearly three hundred times in the Bible. It is essentially a legal term, meaning "contract," and is used for various formal agreements concerning international relations, slavery, and marriage. When the biblical writers use the term covenant to describe the relationship between Yahweh and Israel, they have these analogues in mind: thus, God is understood as Israel's king, its suzerain, and worshipping other gods is a kind of treason or disloyalty. Likewise, God is Israel's owner—the Israelites, collectively, are his slaves, required to obey his commands. And, in an analogy used especially by the prophets, God is Israel's husband, and as in a marriage, this is an exclusive relationship, so that worshipping other gods is like adultery. Importantly, although various types of contracts are known from the ancient Near East, there is no nonbiblical use of this legal model to characterize the relationship between a deity and a people.

God makes covenants with several individuals and groups in the Bible, including those with Noah and his offspring, Abraham and his offspring, and, later, with King David and his dynasty. The most important, however, is the covenant between God and Israel at Mount Sinai.

The text of this contract or covenant is the most famous of the several ancient Israelite law codes or collections: the Ten Commandments or the Decalogue, the latter being a more accurate translation of what the Hebrew Bible calls the "ten words"

The Ten Commandments

I am the LORD your God, who brought you out of the land of Egypt, out of the house of slavery; you shall have no other gods before me.

You shall not make for yourself a statue, or any image of what is in heaven above, or on the earth beneath, or in the water under the earth. You shall not bow down to them or worship them; for I the LORD your God am a jealous God, punishing sons for the iniquity of fathers, to the third and the fourth generation of those who reject me, but showing steadfast love to the thousandth generation of those who love me and keep my commandments.

You shall not make wrongful use of the name of the LORD your God, for the LORD will not acquit anyone who misuses his name.

Remember the sabbath day, and keep it holy. Six days you shall labor and do all your work. But the seventh day is a sabbath to the LORD your God; you shall not do any work—you, your son or your daughter, your male or female slave, your livestock, or your alien inside your gates. For in six days the LORD made heaven and earth, the sea, and all that is in them, but rested the seventh day; therefore the LORD blessed the sabbath day and consecrated it.

Honor your father and your mother, so that your days may be long in the land that the LORD your God is giving you.

You shall not murder.

You shall not commit adultery.

You shall not kidnap.

You shall not bear false witness against your neighbor.

You shall not covet your neighbor's house; you shall not covet your neighbor's wife, or his male or female slave, or his ox, or his donkey, or anything that belongs to your neighbor. (Exod. 20:2–17)

(Deut. 4:13). The two tablets on which the Decalogue was written were stored in the ark of the covenant.

This version of the Decalogue in the preceding box is that found in Exodus 20. But there are two other versions of the Decalogue in the Bible. A second is in Deuteronomy 5, in the context of a lengthy speech given by Moses just before his death, as the Israelites are poised to enter the Promised Land. In that speech Moses reviews the events of the preceding forty years of wandering, from the Exodus onward, and reminds the Israelites of the laws that they had been given by God. Those laws, however, are not always identical to the ones found earlier in Exodus, and there are about twenty, mostly minor, differences between the version of the Decalogue in Exodus and that in Deuteronomy. The most significant concerns the motivation for keeping the Sabbath. In Deuteronomy it is humanitarian—"so that your male and female slave may rest as well as you. Remember that you were slaves in the land of Egypt." (Deut. 5:14–15), whereas in Exodus it is in imitation of the divine rest after creation—"for in six days the LORD made heaven and earth, the sea, and all that is in them, but rested the seventh day" (Exod. 20:11).

A third version of the Decalogue is found in Exodus 34:11–26. According to the narrative, when Moses came down from Mount Sinai to find the Israelites cavorting around the golden calf, he was so angry that he smashed the two tablets on which God had written the Decalogue. So, after punishing some of the perpetrators, Moses had to go back up the mountain for a replacement set. But this version is a very different set of "ten words" (Exod. 34:28), entirely concerned with proper and improper worship, which is why scholars refer to it as the Ritual Decalogue.

There were thus several versions of the Ten Commandments used in ancient Israel at various times and in various places, and, wishing to preserve them despite their inconsistencies, the editors of the Bible took advantage of the plot to include the Ritual Decalogue. These different versions are another illustration of how various sources are incorporated into the final version of the Bible. Even the version found in Exodus 20 has its own literary history: it starts off with Yahweh speaking in the first person, but then shifts to the third person after the first two commandments, probably because of later expansions.

Like the Covenant Code, the Decalogue originated in an agricultural and essentially patriarchal society. Addressed to individual adult males, who preside over a household comprising wife, sons and daughters, slaves, livestock, and resident aliens, the Decalogue only hints at a slightly higher status for women with the mention of "father *and* mother" (Exod. 20:12). The frequent modern appeal to the Ten Commandments as a timeless moral code blithely ignores its original context and some of the questionable values it incorporates.

The Decalogue divides naturally into two parts, which specify the Israelites' obligations to God and to each other. The first part begins by requiring the worship of Yahweh alone. This prohibition of worshipping other gods is not strictly monotheistic—in fact, the commandment presumes that other gods exist but prohibits the Israelites from worshipping them. Moreover, that worship is to be different from the ways in which other people worship their deities: there are to be no representations of God, or for that matter of any other divine, human, or animal form, and the sacred personal name of God, Yahweh, is not to be used in magic, sorcery, or other unlawful ways, for Yahweh is not a deity who can be localized or controlled. And finally, and somewhat mysteriously because there are no good parallels to the Sabbath elsewhere in the ancient Near East, the Israelites are to observe the seventh day of each week as a solemn day of rest.

The second part of the Decalogue details the obligations of Israelite males toward their fellow Israelites, that is, their "neighbors." Parents are to be honored even in old age, and a man's life, his marriage, his person, his legal standing, and his property must be scrupulously respected. If they abide by these rules, then their "days will be long in the land that Yahweh . . . is giving" them (Exod. 20:12). This covenant, then, is conditional: continued possession of the land and prosperity in it depend upon observance of the terms of the agreement.

Biblical writers do not distinguish obligations to God from those to members of the community. Whereas we might separate religious obligations from criminal and civil law, the Decalogue, and biblical laws in general, do not do so. All of the commandments were divinely given, and so violation of any of them was an offense against God, who was their author and also the creator of the community that had pledged itself to him. Put mythologically, the "tablets . . . were written with the finger of God" (Exod. 31:18).

Appropriately, then, many sections of the various legal collections described have to do not only with strictly legal matters but also with religious obligations, including detailed prescriptions for various rituals, such as different kinds of sacrifices and the observance of holy days. The intermingling of these two categories is another illustration of the considerable overlap between sacred and secular—or rather, the lack of distinction between them.

Chapter 7

"Festivals of the LORD": ritual in ancient Israel

Someone with the ambition to read the Bible in its entirety often starts at the beginning, in Genesis, and moves along without much difficulty until the second half of the book of Exodus. At that point the reader may become bogged down and abandon the project because of the numbing details of the many divinely given regulations concerning sacred objects, holy days, priests, sacrifices, and matters such as cleanness and uncleanness.

Such details are present partly because priests were responsible for the final form of the first five books of the Bible, the Torah. Not surprisingly, the ancient priests meticulously, even lovingly, catalogued a bewildering variety of specifics, setting down for posterity both a record of religious rituals practiced in Israel at different times and also an idealized version of how they wanted them to be carried out in the future.

But details concerning religious observance, both public and private, are not restricted to the books of Exodus, Leviticus, Numbers, and Deuteronomy. Throughout the Bible, there are references to various rituals and festivals. Every society has such stylized actions and ceremonies that mark moments perceived as important.

Some of these have to do with the human life cycle. Thus, the Bible refers to rituals concerning birth, puberty and marriage, and death. In connection with birth there are naming ceremonies and, in later periods at least, circumcision, although that was likely originally a puberty ritual. The Bible refers repeatedly to marriage, but there are few accounts of actual marriage ceremonies; Psalm 45 is a hymn for a royal wedding. There are accounts of mourning rituals as well, including fasting, symbolic self-mutilation, lamentation, and burial. The Bible gives us only scattered information about such rituals in ancient Israel, presumably because they were performed in the home and the priests who codified the ritual regulations of the Torah were understandably more interested in those rituals in which they themselves played a primary role.

Priests

Most of the rituals described in the Bible are under the charge of various classes of priests. The structure of this inherited male hierarchy changed over the centuries, but one constant is its restriction to the tribe of Levi and, eventually, to one branch of that tribe that traced its ancestry back to Moses's brother Aaron, who in the Exodus narrative is presented as the first high priest.

These priests were what anthropologists call ritual specialists. Like other professionals, such as prophets and scribes, priests were rigorously trained, and they guarded their expertise jealously. That expertise was wide reaching. Priests were first and foremost responsible for the sacrifices offered by the laity on a daily, seasonal, and occasional basis, sacrifices of which the priests received a share that was their principal means of support. These offerings are described in great detail in the Bible, categorized into different types for different occasions.

Some offerings were made to remedy "uncleanness" or ritual impurity, which could be caused by disease, and so the priests

Sacrificial ritual: an example

The LORD spoke to Moses, saying: Speak to the people of Israel, saying: Anyone who would offer to the LORD a sacrifice of well-being must himself bring to the LORD his offering from his sacrifice of well-being. His own hands shall bring the LORD's offering by fire; he shall bring the fat with the breast, so that the breast may be raised as an elevation offering before the LORD. The priest shall turn the fat into smoke on the altar, but the breast shall belong to Aaron and his sons. And the right thigh from your sacrifices of well-being you shall give to the priest as an offering; the one among the sons of Aaron who offers the blood and fat of the offering of well-being shall have the right thigh for a portion. For I have taken the breast of the elevation offering, and the thigh that is offered, from the people of Israel, from their sacrifices of well-being, and have given them to Aaron the priest and to his sons, as a perpetual due from the Israelites. (Lev. 7:28–34)

functioned as health care providers as well. Priests were also called upon to resolve legal issues and otherwise to interpret the divine will, especially through their use of divination.

The ritual calendar

The three principal religious festivals in ancient Israel were originally regional celebrations, held at a local shrine to which the participants would travel. The Hebrew word used for these festivals literally means "pilgrimage" (*hag*, a word related to Arabic *hajj*, used for the Muslim pilgrimage to Mecca). They were also linked to the agricultural cycle. In the early spring there was the festival of unleavened bread, which occurred at the time of the harvest of barley that had been planted in the late fall. Another early spring festival, known as the Passover, involved the sacrifice of a newly born lamb. These two festivals came from separate socioeconomic contexts, those of farmers and herders, but were joined at a relatively early stage.

A second festival was the festival of weeks (Hebrew *Shavuot*), coinciding with the harvest of winter wheat, occurring seven weeks (fifty days) after Passover. This holy day was also called "festival of harvest" (Exod. 23:16) or "first fruits" (Num. 28:26), and is later known as Pentecost, from the Greek word for "fifty."

Completing the cycle of agricultural festivals was the "festival of ingathering" (Exod. 23:16), which took place at the time of the harvest of grapes, olives, and other fruits in the early fall, in the seventh month. It is also known as the festival of booths (or tabernacles; Hebrew *Sukkot*), probably because the harvesters, whether members of the household or hired laborers, spent the night in the fields in temporary structures. The Bible also mentions in passing a "day of atonement" (Lev. 23:27–28; 25:9), also observed in the seventh month, apparently a ritual of cleansing to prepare the sanctuary, the priests, and the community as a whole for the fall harvest festival; as Yom Kippur this holy day becomes much more important in subsequent Jewish tradition.

With this background in mind, let us imagine that we are at a local shrine, where males, if not families, from miles around have gathered to celebrate a successful harvest. As the worshippers approach the shrine, they sing hymns, punctuated by the bleating of sheep and goats that will be sacrificed. They present them to a priest wearing colorful vestments. He burns an incense offering, whose aromatic smoke fills the air and also masks the stench of the animal slaughter that follows. Throughout the ceremony, more hymns are sung, accompanied by all sorts of musical instruments. The mood is joyful, and as the ritual takes place there are sights and sounds and smells that make for a lively, even chaotic scene.

7. An eighth-century BCE ceramic figurine, about 8.5 inches tall, of a woman playing a drum. It illustrates one way that women participated in worship in ancient Israel.

The ritual calendar included other observances, each of which has its own history. There were daily offerings, weekly offerings on the Sabbath, and offerings at the appearance of the new moon. As Jewish tradition continued, other holy days were added, such as Hanukkah, at the time of the winter solstice, associated with the rededication of the Temple in the second century BCE after the successful revolt of the Maccabees against Greek rule, and Purim, celebrated in the late winter, probably originally a Babylonian ritual assimilated into Judaism and legitimated in the biblical book of Esther.

Passover

The important festival of the Passover, which commemorates the Exodus from Egypt, provides an example of the complicated history of ancient Israelite rituals. In postbiblical Jewish tradition the Passover is celebrated in the home, and that is how it is described in Exodus 12:3–8. But other texts indicate that in some periods the Passover, like the festivals of weeks (*Shavuot*) and booths (*Sukkot*), was celebrated at a central location, either a regional shrine or the national temple in Jerusalem. Jerusalem is where pilgrims from all over Israel reportedly came to celebrate the Passover during the reigns of Hezekiah in the late eighth century BCE and Josiah in the late seventh, as well as in the first century CE according to the Gospels of the New Testament and other sources.

Passover is celebrated for a week in the spring, beginning on the fourteenth day of the first month (Exod. 12:18; Lev. 23:5). A fall new year, in which the first month occurs in the fall, is also attested, which eventually became the Jewish holy day of Rosh Hashanah (literally, "the beginning of the year"). The new year thus seems to have been celebrated in the spring in some periods and in the fall in others.

The terminology for the spring holy day is revealing. In two very early ritual calendars it is called the "festival of unleavened bread" (Exod. 23:15; 34:18), and in both of these it is listed along with the two other pilgrimage festivals. Like them, the festival of unleavened bread is connected with the agricultural cycle, in this case with the early spring barley harvest. This festival was therefore a farmers' ritual, who would bring to their local shrine a portion of their crop as an offering. In slightly later texts, it is combined with the holy day called the Passover (Hebrew *pesah*), as in Leviticus 23:5–6: "In the first month, on the fourteenth day of the month, at twilight, there shall be a passover offering to the LORD, and on the fifteenth day of the same month is the festival of unleavened bread to the LORD; seven days you shall eat unleavened bread." The originally separate holy day of Passover featured the slaughter of a young lamb and presumably was a sheep-herders' ritual.

The core meaning of the word *pesah* is probably "protection." The slaughter of the lamb in the spring was a sacrifice to secure divine protection for flocks and their owners. There is another possible meaning, however, conveniently rendered in English as Passover: because the Israelites smeared the blood of lambs on their door frames, Yahweh passed over their houses when he crossed (that is, passed over) the land of Egypt.

The second meaning points to how the combined festivals of unleavened bread and Passover became associated with the narrative of the Exodus. Different biblical sources do not, however, connect the festivals with the Exodus in the same ways. While the earliest ritual calendars refer only to the date—"You shall keep the festival of unleavened bread. Seven days you shall eat unleavened bread, as I commanded you, at the time appointed in the month of Abib; for in the month of Abib you came out from Egypt" (Exod. 34:18), another text links more than just the chronology—it is unleavened bread that is eaten because the Israelites left Egypt so quickly that they had no time to let their bread rise (Exod. 12:39). The bread, originally unleavened to keep it pure rather than contaminated with old yeast in the form of starter dough, is called "the bread of affliction—because you came out of the land of Egypt in great haste" (Deut. 16:3). Likewise, the sacrifice of the lamb as a substitution for the firstborn, as in the story of the sacrifice of Isaac (Gen. 22) and in the Ritual Decalogue (Exod. 34:18–19), is connected with the killing of the firstborn of the Egyptians.

Thus the festivals of unleavened bread and Passover were originally independent rituals that were joined at a fairly early stage, and both were linked with the narrative of the Exodus. This process of linkage continued in Jewish tradition as the Passover service developed over the ages. For example, the typical modern Passover Seder or meal includes *haroset,* a blend of fruits, nuts, and spices that represents the mortar the Israelite slaves used when laying bricks, and *karpas,* green herbs dipped in salt water that recalls their bitter service.

The same linking of originally seasonal festivals with the Exodus occurs with the other two pilgrimage festivals, those of weeks (*Shavuot*) and booths (*Sukkot*). In early biblical texts they are simply agricultural: "You shall observe the festival of weeks, the first fruits of wheat harvest, and the festival of ingathering at the turn of the year" (Exod. 34:22). In postbiblical Jewish tradition the festival of weeks becomes a commemoration of the giving of the law on Mount Sinai; and even before the end of the biblical period the fall harvest festival of ingathering, also called booths, recalls the temporary structures that the Israelites lived in during the forty years of wandering in the wilderness after the Exodus (Lev. 23:42).

According to Exodus 12:43–49, the Passover observance was limited to circumcised members of the Israelite community. Foreigners and slaves who wished to participate had to have been circumcised. This seems at odds with the understanding of Passover as a family ritual but is consistent with the later development of the Passover as a national pilgrimage festival in which only males participated. To this minimal requirement, the book of Numbers adds another, that of ritual purity, a concept that pervades biblical laws.

Pure and impure

According to Numbers 9:10–13, those who are unable to
celebrate the Passover at the appointed time should do so a month
later. Two reasons for such a delay are given: the person is on a
journey, or he has touched a corpse. Contact with corpses caused
ritual impurity, so much so that a high priest was not permitted to
touch the dead, even those in his own family. Much of the
legislation found in the books of Leviticus and Numbers has to do
with the categories of purity and impurity, often misleadingly
translated as "cleanness" and "uncleanness." These categories
constitute two distinct conditions pertaining to persons and also to
animals, houses, clothing, and food: purity was a prerequisite for
participation or use in ritual, and impurity barred them.

The origins of the distinction are unclear. Some forms of impurity
may reflect an awareness of contagion: a skin disease or an
unnatural bodily emission made a person impure, and he or she
had to be quarantined until a priest had certified that the person
was no longer impure and had made the required offering. Others
may have to do with primal taboos, especially concerning sex and
death. Seminal emission, menstruation, and childbirth all made a
person impure, as did touching a dead person or animal. Other
explanations are also possible and not necessarily mutually
exclusive.

Foods were also classified as pure and impure. Diet is one way that
a culture differentiates itself from others, and avoiding some foods,
such as pork, may have originated in this way. Other prohibitions
may be related to a sense of order: a field was not to be sown with
different species of seeds, and linen and wool were not to be woven
into one fabric.

The result was an all-encompassing system, over which the priests
presided. They determined when a person's impurity had passed,
and they received as payment a share of the sacrifices offered.

Sacred songs

Scattered throughout the narrative books of the Bible are dozens of hymns. There are victory hymns, such as that sung by Miriam and the women after the Exodus from Egypt; laments, such as those intoned by David after the deaths of persons close to him; prayers for divine forgiveness; and other types as well.

A few hymns found in the narrative books also occur in the book of Psalms, the longest book of the Bible, and so not surprisingly one of the most complex. It is in essence the hymnbook of ancient Israel, containing hymns originally from different shrines and from different times, collected relatively late in the biblical period. There are more than a dozen different types or genres of these hymns, all of which were presumably set to music. The most common is the individual lament, in which a person in difficulty asks for divine assistance, expressing confidence that the prayer will be heard and anticipating the expression of gratitude when it has been. Different components of the genre of the individual lament, such as trust and giving thanks, can become hymns in their own right. There are also communal laments and hymns in praise of Yahweh as creator and as Israel's king and helper. Because most of the psalms have no specific historical references, they are difficult to date. This accounts for their continuing use in worship by both Jews and Christians over the ages.

Chapter 8
Prophets and prophecies

Many individuals are identified in the Bible as prophets, and some fifteen books of the Bible are named for prophets. In modern English, a prophet is commonly thought of as a person who predicts the future. That is part of the biblical understanding of prophecy but not its primary meaning, which is that prophets were intermediaries between God and humans. Thus, although Moses is not usually described as forecasting the future, he is the biblical prophet par excellence. The same understanding is found in the offshoots of ancient Judaism: in Christianity, both Moses and Jesus are prophets; and in Islam, Moses, Jesus, and Muhammad have the same title. These founding prophets were not primarily prognosticators. Rather, they were individuals who relayed divine messages to their followers.

This meaning is illustrated by a metaphorical use of the term prophet:

> Yahweh said to Moses, "See, I have made you like God to Pharaoh, and your brother Aaron shall be your prophet. You shall speak all that I command you, and your brother Aaron shall tell Pharaoh to let the Israelites go out of his land. (Exod. 7:1–2)

In this analogy, Moses is like God, Aaron is his spokesperson or prophet, and Pharaoh is the audience: the prophet, then, is the go-between. The Greek word from which "prophet" is derived means someone who speaks for someone else, and more specifically an interpreter of a divinely given message.

Discerning the divine

For almost everyone in prescientific ages, and for some people even today, many events were understood as caused by the ruling power(s) of the universe. Thus earthquakes, famines, and droughts were not considered natural disasters—rather, they were supernatural, caused by a god or gods. The same explanation was provided for other experiences, including dreams, the movement of the heavenly bodies, and even such apparently random phenomena as the shape of clouds or the pattern of a flock of birds in flight. The interpretation of such phenomena is, appropriately, called divination.

The book of Ezekiel describes the Babylonian king Nebuchadrezzar as he prepared to attack Jerusalem in the early sixth century BCE:

> The king of Babylon stands at the parting of the way, at the fork in the two roads, to use divination; he shakes the arrows, he consults the teraphim, he inspects the liver. Into his right hand comes the lot for Jerusalem. (Ezek. 21:21–22)

Using several methods, Nebuchadrezzar seems to be seeking divine guidance about his military strategy, just as kings of Israel are reported to have consulted God through prophets and other means about the advisability of going into battle. From ancient Mesopotamia come many thousands of clay models of animal livers inscribed with directions for interpreting them. These omen texts, as they are called, explain the phrase "inspecting the liver." Other types of divination attributed to Nebuchadrezzar are found in the Bible. For example, the prophet Elisha uses arrows to predict a series of royal victories (2 Kings 13:14–19). There are frequent

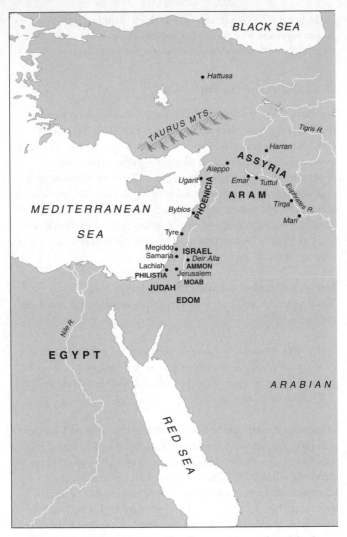

8. **Map of the ancient Near East.** *Prophets are reported at cities in italics.*

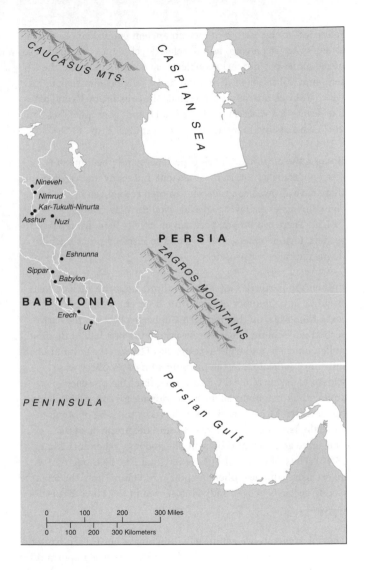

references to the casting of lots, an ancient equivalent of drawing straws or tossing a coin, and to related techniques that made use of the somewhat mysterious objects called the ephod and the teraphim. All forms of divination had a religious dimension, in which Yahweh answered individuals "by dreams, by Urim [dice-like devices associated with the ephod], and by prophets" (1 Sam. 28:6), and casting lots put an end to disputes (Prov. 18:18).

Because the meaning of such experiences and phenomena is often not transparent, in most ancient and many modern societies there have always been men and women recognized by their contemporaries as having special, even divinely given, insight. There is a broad spectrum of activity here, from palm readers, fortune tellers, and psychics to inspired proclaimers of divine messages, or prophets.

Prophets in particular are attested throughout the ancient Near East in a large number of texts from different periods. These texts, from Mari on the northern Euphrates River in the early second millennium BCE, from Assyria in the first half of the first millennium BCE, and from a scattering of sites in the Levant in both millennia, indicate that the phenomenon of prophecy was widespread. The biblical writers recognized the presence among their neighbors of such individuals, for example Balaam, the northern Mesopotamian seer hired by the king of Moab to curse the Israelites (Num. 22–24), and the prophets of the Canaanite god Baal and his wife the goddess Asherah (1 Kings 18:19). Thus, although prophecy might at first be thought of as an exclusively biblical phenomenon, a revelation from the one true God to specially chosen individuals, even in the Bible that is not the case.

The fullest picture we get of such individuals, however, is from the Bible, partly because prophets and prophecy were so important for the biblical writers, and presumably for their audiences and ancient Israelite society in general. In the Old Testament, several

An ancient Mesopotamian prophet

This is an excerpt from a letter from Nur-Sin, an ambassador of Zimri-Lim, the king of Mari on the Euphrates in the eighteenth century BCE:

> A prophet of [the storm god] Adad, lord of Aleppo, came with Abu-halim and spoke to him as follows: "Am I not Adad, lord of Aleppo, who raised you in my lap and restored you to your ancestral throne? I do not demand anything from you. When a wronged man or woman cries out to you, be there and judge their case. This only I have demanded from you. If you do what I have written to you and heed my word, I will give you the land from the rising of the sun to its setting, your land greatly increased." This is what the prophet of Adad, lord of Aleppo, said in the presence of Abu-halim. My lord should know this.[1]

This oracle guaranteeing divine support for the ruler resembles that attributed to the prophet Nathan, when he proclaimed Yahweh's promise to King David that his descendants would rule forever (2 Sam. 7:4–17).

dozen men and women are named as prophets, and many more are unnamed. As elsewhere in the ancient world, they functioned in a variety of ways. A "seer" or a "man of God" could help find something that had been lost, and alongside prophets the Bible also mentions soothsayers, diviners, augurs, those who cast spells, and those who consult ghosts or spirits. Although many of these activities were banned, some by the religious reform of the Judean king Josiah in the late seventh century BCE, the frequent references to them indicate that they were widespread in ancient Israel.

Such individuals, like saints, shamans, and mystics in many religions, were sometimes on the margins of society, in part because of their unconventional behavior. In both biblical and nonbiblical sources there are examples of prophets entering ecstatic states prior to delivering their message. When the newly anointed King Saul "prophesied," he became "another man" (1 Sam. 10:6). Sometimes that ecstatic state was reached by means of music (1 Sam. 10:5; 2 Kings 3:15), and it could involve nakedness (1 Sam. 19:24) or self-mutilation (1 Kings 18:28; Zech. 13:6). Other abnormal behavior is reported, for example, of the prophet Ezekiel, including speechlessness and lying on one side for a long time.

As is also true of such persons in other cultures, in the Bible there are legends about prophets' miraculous abilities. This is especially true of the prophets Elijah and Elisha, who are reported to have multiplied food, healed the sick, raised the dead, rendered poison harmless, and even made a lost iron axe head float to the surface after it had sunk in the Jordan River. They could also draw on divine power—calling fire from heaven, or bears from the woods to maul rude boys. Their power continued even after their deaths—Elisha's bones, for example, restored a corpse to life. Similar miraculous activity is also reported of later prophets, such as Isaiah, who was able to make a shadow cast by the sun reverse direction, and who was also a healer.

Not all prophets were on the periphery of society. Among the biblical prophets for whom we are given biographical details, Amos was a farmer, and Jeremiah and Ezekiel were priests. Throughout the ancient Near East, including Israel, many prophets were associated with ruling monarchs. Since much of ancient Near Eastern literature is a product of the elite in royal courts, it is difficult to know what percentage of prophets were royal appointees or clients. Some biblical prophets seem to have served as official or semi-official royal advisors, such as Gad, Nathan, Isaiah, and Jeremiah. Many are also reported to have been involved in the selection and even the coronation of kings, such as Elijah, Nathan, Ahijah, and probably Isaiah. At the same time, because their authority was viewed as divinely given, they often criticized kings in the name of God.

Some prophets were professionals, trained by a period of apprenticeship under a master prophet. He was their "father" (see 2 Kings 2:12; 13:14), and they were the "sons of the prophet" (2 Kings 4:38). Others apparently were amateurs, like the prophet Amos, who asserted:

> I am not a prophet, nor a son of a prophet; but I am a herder, and a dresser of sycamore trees, and Yahweh took me from following the flock, and Yahweh said to me, "Go, prophesy to my people Israel." (Amos 7:14–15)

Here Amos claims that despite his lack of professional training he is a true prophet, because he received a call.

Modes of revelation

The prophets believed, as did their contemporaries, that they received direct and special communication from the divine. Speech and vision are the most frequent metaphors used to describe such communication—the prophets were both hearers and seers. The non-Israelite seer Balaam, for example, describes himself as "one who hears the words of God, who sees the vision of the Almighty" (Num. 24:4). Likewise, the opening of the book of the prophet Amos mentions "the words of Amos . . . which he saw" (Amos 1:1). A standard formula for revelation to prophets is that "the word of the LORD came to" them; then the prophet speaks, not in his or her own name, but in the name of Yahweh: "Thus says the LORD." In scholarly jargon, the message that the prophet delivered is called an oracle, a term derived from classical antiquity.

But how exactly did the prophets receive their messages? One form of revelation was dreams, and there is a widely attested process called incubation, in which an individual would spend the night in a sacred place precisely in order to have an inspired dream. Were their accounts of divine revelation the vivid externalization of a profound inner experience, or did they actually see or hear anything? A modern critical understanding suggests that they did not, but in any case what was significant was the inner experience, as well as the shared conviction among prophets and their audiences that the experience was divinely given.

One of the most significant recurring accounts of revelation is the claim by some prophets to have witnessed, or even participated in, the deliberations of the assembly of the gods, the divine council

Isaiah's vision

In this first-person narrative, the prophet Isaiah describes his participation in the divine council, during which he is commissioned to prophesy to God's people:

> In the year that King Uzziah died, I saw the Lord sitting on a throne, high and lofty; and the hem of his robe filled the temple. Seraphs were in attendance above him; each had six wings: with two they covered their faces, and with two they covered their feet, and with two they flew. And one called to another and said:
>
> > "Holy, holy, holy is Yahweh of hosts;
> > the whole earth is full of his glory." . . .
>
> Then I heard the voice of the Lord saying, "Whom shall I send, and who will go for us?" And I said, "Here am I; send me!" And he said, "Go and say to this people:
>
> > 'Keep listening, but do not comprehend;
> > keep looking, but do not understand.' " (Isa. 6:1-3, 8-9)

over which in ancient Israelite religion Yahweh presided. For example, the prophet Micaiah reports: "I saw Yahweh sitting on his throne, with all the host of heaven standing beside him to his right and to his left" (1 Kings 22:19). Likewise, Jeremiah claims that only he, and not the false prophets, had stood in the divine council (Jer. 23:22).

Classical prophecy

Prophets appear frequently in biblical narratives set before the eighth century BCE. The accounts concerning them are often legendary and in the books of Samuel and Kings have been incorporated into the Former Prophets of Jewish tradition. Beginning in the eighth century BCE, however, we encounter a new kind of prophecy, or at least a new genre of prophetic expression. This is found in the writing prophets, or the classical prophets, whose words were collected and preserved in the books known as the Latter Prophets, that is, the lengthy books of Isaiah, Jeremiah, and Ezekiel, the Major Prophets, and the shorter books of Hosea through Malachi, the twelve Minor Prophets.

At least two factors contributed to this development. One was the spread of literacy in ancient Israel, which enabled the oracles of prophets to be written down and collected, either by the prophets themselves or by their followers. A second factor was the Israelites' growing engagement with and eventual subjugation to major powers of the Near East, especially the Assyrians in the eighth and seventh centuries BCE, and their successors the Babylonians in the late seventh and early sixth centuries. The divided kingdoms of Israel in the north and Judah in the south, directly in the path of the Assyrians and later the Babylonians in their imperial advances, especially toward Egypt, were no match for those superpowers, and the prophets were important interpreters of these events.

The prophetic books generally include two different types of material. One is prophetic oracles, the speeches given by the prophets, often in poetry. A second type of material in the prophetic books is prose narratives, either autobiographical, in which the prophet describes his own experiences, or biographical, in which details of the prophet's career are recounted by others. It is often difficult to determine how these different materials were organized. A few books, such as Ezekiel and Haggai, have precise dates and a chronological order, but many of the others have no obvious principle of arrangement. Furthermore, most of them, especially the longer ones, have their own literary history, a history of arrangement, editing, and additions.

As an example of the complicated nature of the prophetic books, consider the relatively short book of Amos, the earliest of the classical prophets. It opens, as do most of the prophetic books, with a historical note about the prophet. There follows a short oracle, in which the prophet announces Yahweh's judgment; this same oracle also occurs in Joel, and such duplication of material in the prophetic books is not uncommon. The first major unit in the book of Amos is a carefully patterned series of oracles in which Yahweh first announces his judgment on the nations surrounding Israel and then on Israel itself. Then follow, with no discernible principle of arrangement, an oracle on the nature of prophecy; several oracles against Israel and groups within it, especially the elite in the royal capitals of Samaria and Jerusalem; snippets of hymns; oracles of woe; first-person narratives in which the prophet describes a series of visions (although these are not all grouped together); a third-person prose narrative about the prophet; and an oracle promising divine restoration of the dynasty founded by David but now apparently fallen. And all of this in only nine chapters!

Amos was active in the mid-eighth century BCE, a period of relative autonomy and prosperity in the small kingdoms of the Levant, such as Israel, Judah, Aram-Damascus, Ammon, Moab, and Tyre. The Assyrians, whose imperial expansion had begun in earnest in the ninth century, were for a few decades preoccupied with troubles on their northern and southern borders, and so the states of the western Levant had a brief respite. But the Assyrian advance would shortly resume. In his oracles, Amos anticipated this resurgence of Assyrian aggression and its consequences.

The policy of the Assyrians toward a conquered territory was well known. They generally removed the ruling family from power, frequently destroyed the capital and other major cities, and deported many of the elite to other areas of their empire, replacing them with colonists transplanted from other regions into what became an Assyrian province ruled by a governor appointed by the Assyrian king. This is precisely what Amos announced. In the case of Damascus, for example, the capital would be destroyed, along with other royal strongholds, the ruling family removed, and the people sent into exile (Amos 1:4–5). Similar actions are announced for other neighbors of the Israelites, and for both Israel and Judah, whose aristocracy in the capitals of Samaria and Jerusalem would be exiled (Amos 6:1, 7; 7:11).

That was what happened. The Assyrians captured and destroyed Damascus in 732 BCE and Samaria in 722, and both became Assyrian provinces. Judah had become an Assyrian vassal in 734, and so the Assyrians left Judah alone for a time, but when it too proved rebellious, the Assyrian army laid siege to Jerusalem in 701. So, in a sense, Amos had predicted what would occur. But it would not have taken a special divine revelation to anticipate the actions of the Assyrians, and later of their successors the Babylonians. What is noteworthy about Amos 1–2 and similar texts is not their apparently predictive quality. Rather, it is the interpretation, the spin as it were, that they give to the anticipated Assyrian advance. From a modern historical perspective, the Assyrian conquests were the inevitable result of the vast superiority of a military superpower to relatively small states that stood in its way. But for Amos and the prophets who followed him, including Hosea, Isaiah, Micah, and Jeremiah, such an explanation was insufficient. Amos repeatedly asserts that Yahweh himself was responsible:

I will take you into exile beyond Damascus. (Amos 5:27)

I will deliver up the city and all that is in it. (6:8)

I am raising up against you a nation,

O house of Israel, says the LORD, the God of hosts. (6:14)

Amos, like the biblical prophets in general, insisted on the divine control of human history: the defeat of kings, cities, and nations was ultimately due to divine activity. Yahweh was angry with his people, and he used the imperial powers of his day to punish them for their failure to observe their covenant with him. This was the insight of the prophets, their interpretation of the events of their times.

Messengers of the covenant

Underlying the immediate involvement of the prophets in the particulars of their own times, then, there is a consistent message. What had happened, what was happening, and what would happen were all the doing of Yahweh. He was "the lord of all the earth" (Ps. 97:5), and thus responsible for events throughout the entire world, not just within Israel's borders. But his primary focus was Israel, his chosen people.

The Israelites had made a covenant with God at Mount Sinai, but they had broken that agreement. The primary text of the covenant is the Ten Commandments, whose obligations fall into two categories: exclusive worship of Yahweh alone, in the manner he prescribed, and concern for their fellow Israelites. Keeping these obligations brought divine blessing, and failure to do so brought divine punishment. The reward was continued prosperity in the land that Yahweh had given them, and the punishment could take many forms—drought, famine, and especially enemy attack, defeat, and even exile.

So whether it was Amos in the mid-eighth century BCE, or Isaiah a few decades later, or Jeremiah in the early sixth century, the prophets were all deeply immersed in their times, which they interpreted from a particular theological perspective: that God was ultimately responsible for their experiences, for weal and for woe, to reward and punish. The prophets proclaimed the divine judgment: they were, in the words of the book of Malachi (3:1), "messengers of the covenant." With remarkable consistency, they condemned the Israelites for their repeated failure to live up to their covenant—by worshipping other gods and not treating each other fairly. At times that condemnation, like the very notion of covenant itself, used a legal analogy, the lawsuit. Speaking through the prophet, Yahweh indicts Israel for breach of contract and announces the punishment that will be imposed:

> Hear the word of the LORD, O people of Israel;
>   for the LORD has an indictment against the inhabitants of the land.
> There is no faithfulness or loyalty,
>   and no knowledge of God in the land.
> Swearing, lying, and murder,
>   and stealing and adultery break out;
>   bloodshed follows bloodshed.
> Therefore the land mourns,
>   and all who live in it languish;
> together with the wild animals
>   and the birds of the air,
>   even the fish of the sea are perishing. (Hosea 4:1–3)

In this passage, the eighth-century prophet Hosea alludes to the Ten Commandments, as does Jeremiah in the late seventh century, urging the Israelites to return to their founding principles:

> For if you truly amend your ways and your doings, if you truly act justly one with another, if you do not oppress the alien, the orphan, and the widow, or shed innocent blood in this place, and if you do not go after other gods to your own hurt, then I will let you dwell in this place, in the land that I gave of old to your ancestors forever and ever.

But you are trusting in lies. Will you steal, murder, commit adultery, swear falsely, make offerings to Baal, and go after other gods that you have not known, and then come and stand before me in this house, which is called by my name, and say, "We are safe!"—only to go on doing all these abominations? (Jer. 7:5–11)

Jeremiah insists that despite the extravagant claim of monarchs of the dynasty founded by David that God would forever protect them and the Temple in their capital Jerusalem, there was a prior commitment—the Sinai Covenant. This was the framework for the prophets' interpretation of the past, the present, and the immediate future. They proclaimed their message in specific historical contexts, to their contemporaries—sometimes individuals, especially kings; sometimes groups within the community; sometimes, at least rhetorically, foreign nations; and most frequently the people of Israel as a whole.

But their message for the most part was not heeded. The Israelites would inevitably receive the punishment that according to the prophets they deserved for their failure to carry out their obligations to love God exclusively and to love their neighbor. And so it happened: the curses attached to the covenant came to pass: their cities were destroyed, they lost control of their land, and they were taken into exile, first from the Northern Kingdom of Israel in 722 BCE, and then from the Southern Kingdom of Judah in the early sixth century BCE.

Prophets and the future

In the aftermath of the destruction of Jerusalem in 586 BCE and the exile to Babylon associated with it, prophecy also took a new twist. There was more and more focus on a future restoration of the glorious days of the past, days of independence and prosperity, especially the time of kings David and Solomon in the tenth century. We find detailed pronouncements of such a future in the prophecies related to the events of the sixth century, especially

Jeremiah, Ezekiel, and Isaiah 40—66, chapters, which although part of the book of Isaiah were written not in his time, the late eighth century, but two centuries later. And, as the prophetic books continued to be revised, expressions of future hope were added to others as well.

But these divinely promised hopes were not immediately fulfilled, and so they were projected into a distant future, an "end time" in

Future hope

The end of the book of Amos is an example of how ideas of restoration of past glory and of future prosperity were added to earlier prophetic books:

> On that day I will raise up
>   the booth of David that is fallen,
> and repair its breaches,
>   and raise up its ruins,
>   and rebuild it as in the days of old . . .
>   says the LORD who does this.
> The time is surely coming, says the LORD,
>   when the one who plows shall overtake the one who reaps,
>   and the treader of grapes the one who sows the seed;
> the mountains shall drip sweet wine,
>   and all the hills shall flow with it.
> I will restore the fortunes of my people Israel,
>   and they shall rebuild the ruined cities and inhabit them;
> they shall plant vineyards and drink their wine,
>   and they shall make gardens and eat their fruit.
> I will plant them upon their land,
>   and they shall never again be plucked up
>   out of the land that I have given them,
>   says the LORD your God. (Amos 9:11–15)

which Yahweh and his heavenly armies would definitively defeat the forces of evil, both primeval and historical. This led to the development of what is known as apocalyptic literature, occurring in the Bible in an early stage in Ezekiel 40–48 and Zechariah 9–14 and more fully in Daniel 7–12, and, in the New Testament, in the book of Revelation.

The early Christians believed that end time to have arrived in the person of Jesus of Nazareth, and so they interpreted the Old Testament prophets as predictors of his eventual coming, and eventually placed the prophetic books immediately before the New Testament in their arrangement of the canon. That interpretation, however, overlooks the immersion of the prophets in their own times. It may surprise Christian readers to learn that in the Hebrew Bible the title *Messiah* (an English form of a Hebrew word meaning "anointed") is never used of a future leader, only of previous and present ones.

Chapter 9
Hezekiah and Sennacherib: another deep probe

In 701 BCE the Assyrian king Sennacherib attacked the Southern Kingdom of Judah and laid siege to Jerusalem. There is much archaeological evidence for this traumatic event, and it features prominently in the book of Kings and in the book of Isaiah the prophet, as well as in Sennacherib's own records. It is a good case study of the relationship between prophets and the events of their times, and how biblical and nonbiblical sources complement each other.

In the second half of the eighth century BCE, the Assyrian Empire was reaching the zenith of its power. In the inexorable advance of the Assyrians toward Egypt, which they conquered in 671 BCE, they began to take over the smaller states of the Levant that stood in their way and had often been unreliable and even rebellious vassals. Among the casualties were Damascus in 732 and the Northern Kingdom of Israel in 722. Israel's southern neighbor Judah survived, in part because of its relatively remote location, some distance from the main coastal highway, and also because beginning in the 730s the kings of Judah had willingly subjected themselves to Assyria as tribute-paying vassals.

At the very end of the eighth century BCE, however, as Assyria was preoccupied with internal difficulties closer to its homeland, the

Sennacherib's account of the siege of Jerusalem

This excerpt from Sennacherib's first-person account of his campaign of 701 BCE describes his attack on Judah:

> As for Hezekiah, the Judean, who had not submitted to my yoke, I besieged forty-six of his fortified walled cities and surrounding small towns, which were without number. Using packed-down ramps and applying battering rams, infantry attacks by mines, breeches, and siege machines, I conquered them. I took out 200,150 people, young and old, male and female, horses, mules, donkeys, camels, cattle, and sheep, without number, and counted them as spoil. Himself I locked him up within Jerusalem, his royal city, like a bird in a cage. I surrounded him with earthworks, and made it unthinkable for him to exit by the city gate. His cities which I had despoiled, I cut off from his land, and gave them to Mitinti, king of Ashdod, Padi, king of Ekron, and Silli-bel, king of Gaza, and thus diminished his land. I imposed upon him in addition to the former tribute, yearly payment of dues and gifts for my lordship.
>
> He, Hezekiah, was overwhelmed by the awesome splendor of my lordship, and he sent me after my departure to Nineveh, my royal city, his elite troops and his best soldiers, which he had brought into Jerusalem as reinforcements, with 30 talents of gold, 800 talents of silver, choice antimony, large blocks of carnelian, beds (inlaid) with ivory, armchairs (inlaid) with ivory, elephant hides, ivory, ebony-wood, boxwood, garments with multicolored trim, garments of linen, wool (dyed) red-purple and blue-purple, vessels of copper, iron, bronze, and tin, chariots, siege shields, lances, armor, daggers for the belt, bows and arrows, countless trappings and instruments of war, together with his daughters, his palace women, his male and female singers. He (also) dispatched his personal messenger to deliver the tribute and to do obeisance.[1]

A biblical account of Sennacherib's attack

Biblical historians record essentially the same events as Sennacherib's account, confirming the substance of Sennacherib's claims in a brief summary:

> In the fourteenth year of King Hezekiah, King Sennacherib of Assyria came up against all the fortified cities of Judah and captured them. King Hezekiah of Judah sent to the king of Assyria at Lachish, saying, "I have done wrong; withdraw from me; whatever you impose on me I will bear." The king of Assyria demanded of King Hezekiah of Judah three hundred talents of silver and thirty talents of gold. Hezekiah gave him all the silver that was found in the house of the LORD and in the treasuries of the king's house. At that time Hezekiah stripped the gold from the doors of the temple of the LORD, and from the doorposts that King Hezekiah of Judah had overlaid and gave it to the king of Assyria. (2 Kings 18:13–16)

Judean king Hezekiah allied with other regional monarchs, including the Egyptian pharaoh, and rebelled against Assyrian imperial rule. The response of Sennacherib, who had come to power in 705, was swift and harsh. In an extensive campaign in 701 BCE he led his army down the Mediterranean coast, replacing rebellious rulers with more compliant ones and enforcing the payment of tribute. This time Judah did not escape. Its major cities were captured and destroyed, and its capital Jerusalem besieged until Hezekiah surrendered and paid an enormous tribute.

For these events we have an unusually plentiful number of independent sources. These include a lengthy Assyrian account attributed to Sennacherib himself, surviving in multiple copies; a series of stone panels carved in low relief from a room in Sennacherib's palace that show Sennacherib's capture of the southern Judean city of Lachish; extensive archaeological evidence for the massive destruction in Judah and for Hezekiah's extensive preparations for the anticipated siege of Jerusalem; and several biblical accounts incorporated into the books of Kings, Chronicles, and Isaiah. Each of these sources must be interpreted, but on the facts they are in agreement.

Archaeological evidence

Both Sennacherib's own account and that in 2 Kings agree that as part of his campaign, Sennacherib attacked the major fortified cities of Judah in order to eliminate local resistance and the outer defenses of the capital in Jerusalem. At a large number of Judean sites, there are layers of ash and other debris resulting from this campaign. The most well known of these sites is Lachish, for which we also have graphic visual evidence in reliefs depicting its siege and conquest from Sennacherib's royal palace at Nineveh, his capital. The archaeological evidence and the reliefs correlate nicely, confirming the details of the Assyrian onslaught and their military tactics.

In preparation for the anticipated siege of Jerusalem, Hezekiah refortified the city, extending its wall to include a more recently settled district known as the Mishneh, or Second Quarter. Excavations have uncovered parts of this wall, dated to the late eighth century BCE.

Another archaeological datum is a tunnel more than 1,700 feet long that goes under the city of David, the original nucleus of Jerusalem. The tunnel itself has been known to scholars since the early nineteenth century and has been convincingly identified with a construction project sponsored by the Judean king Hezekiah in the late eighth century BCE:

> [Hezekiah] made the pool and the conduit and brought water into the city (2 Kings 20:20);

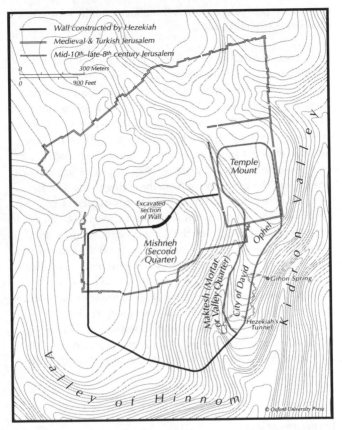

9. **Jerusalem in the late eighth century** BCE.

Hezekiah closed the upper outlet of the waters of Gihon and directed
them down to the west side of the city of David (2 Chron. 32:30).

The tunnel was an aqueduct: it brought the water from the
city's main spring, known appropriately as Gihon ("gusher"),
which was outside the fortifications on the east side, to a newly

constructed pool or reservoir, called Siloam, on the west side, now within the city's wall.

Carved into the wall of the tunnel near its southern end was an inscription. Known as the Siloam Tunnel Inscription, the text is six lines long but is not entirely complete, perhaps because some of it was lost when it was hacked out of the tunnel wall not long after its discovery in 1880. It dramatically describes how two groups of laborers, working deep underground from both ends of the tunnel, met near the center. First they "heard the sound of each man calling to his fellow," and then they met, "pick against pick," whereupon "the water flowed from the spring to the pool for twelve hundred cubits." Although the text is written in an elegant ancient Hebrew script, it does not appear to be an official monument commemorating the tunnel's completion—it does not mention the name of the king who ordered the construction, nor give a date, and its location inside the tunnel is not where one would expect a monumental inscription to be carved. Perhaps it was placed there by the chief engineer or the workers themselves. In any case, almost all scholars agree that the inscription dates to the late eighth century, memorializing this additional phase of preparation for the expected Assyrian siege and dramatically illustrating the short biblical notices.

Interpretation

Sennacherib in other texts presents his victories in religious terms, as gifts from his patron deity Ashur who had designated him as king. Paralleling this ideological interpretation, the biblical sources discuss the events of 701 BCE as ultimately caused by Yahweh, from two distinct perspectives. The first explains the attack itself: Why did Yahweh allow the Assyrians to decimate Judah's defenses and its population? Because Yahweh himself was using them to punish his people for their rebelliousness. Speaking through the prophet Isaiah, Yahweh makes a remarkable assertion:

> Ah, Assyria, the rod of my rage—
>> the staff of my fury!
> Against a godless nation I send him,
>> and against the people with whom I am angry I command him,
> to take spoil and seize plunder,
>> and to tread them down like mud in the streets. (Isa. 10:5–6)

In the prophet's interpretation, the Assyrians were instruments of punishment in Yahweh's hands, because his people had failed to trust in him, but had sought "refuge in the protection of Pharaoh,...shelter in the shadow of Egypt" (Isa. 30:2), that is, they had relied on foreign alliances rather than on Yahweh. Moreover, they had broken their fundamental contract with God, the Sinai Covenant, and so their religious observances were futile until they learned to "seek justice, rescue the oppressed, defend the orphan, plead for the widow" (1:17).

Because the Israelites were rebellious sons (Isa. 1:2, 5), they would be punished. Like a flood coming from the Euphrates River in northern Mesopotamia, their homeland, the Assyrians would inundate Judah (Isa. 8:7–8) with horrific results:

> Your country lies desolate,
>> your cities are burned with fire;
> in your very presence
>> aliens devour your land;
>> it is desolate, as overthrown by foreigners.
> And daughter Zion is left
>> like a booth in a vineyard,
> like a shelter in a cucumber field,
>> like a besieged city. (Isa. 1:7–8)

This is a vivid description of Sennacherib's campaign against Judah and his siege of Jerusalem, reduced to a ramshackle hut in a flattened landscape.

But the story did not end there, for Jerusalem was not captured or destroyed. The matter-of-fact summary in 2 Kings 18:13–16 is followed in 2 Kings 18:17–19:17 by a much lengthier and more ideological account of extended negotiations between Hezekiah and Sennacherib, during which the prophet Isaiah assures Hezekiah that Yahweh will protect Jerusalem for his own sake, and for the sake of his servant David, whose successor Hezekiah is. The account concludes with a verse with a mythical tone:

> That very night the angel of Yahweh set out and struck down one hundred eighty-five thousand in the camp of the Assyrians; when morning dawned, they were all dead bodies. Then King Sennacherib of Assyria left, went home, and lived at Nineveh.
> (2 Kings 19:35)

The Assyrian withdrawal is here interpreted not as the result of Hezekiah's surrender but as direct divine intervention, rewarding Hezekiah's faithfulness and demonstrating Yahweh's guarantee to protect Jerusalem, whose Temple was his home and which was the capital of the dynasty that he himself had chosen.

The historical facts, then, are these: Sennacherib invaded Judea, attacked its major cities, and laid siege to Jerusalem, whereupon Hezekiah surrendered and paid tribute. But those facts were subject to interpretation. Jerusalem had survived, and that was Yahweh's doing, expressed in extravagant terms: a miraculous divine slaughter of the Assyrian army, just as Yahweh had annihilated the Egyptian army during the Exodus from Egypt. So extravagant is this account that both the early second-century BCE writer Sirach and the late first-century CE Jewish historian Josephus demythologized it, attributing the death of Sennacherib's soldiers to a plague. But for Isaiah, and also for the authors of the book of Kings, both Assyria's attack and withdrawal were manifestations of Yahweh's control over history.

This probe illustrates the role of the prophets as interpreters of historical events, informed by their understanding of Yahweh as the most powerful, implicitly even the *only* god. It also provides an example of how, when taken together, biblical and nonbiblical texts and archaeological data mutually enhance our understanding.

Chapter 10
Poetry and dissent

Some of the biblical and nonbiblical texts quoted in this book are
printed in poetic lines, and scholars agree that about a third of
the Old Testament is poetry. But to conserve writing materials
such as papyrus and parchment, in ancient manuscripts poetry and
prose were written the same way, in continuous lines. This is one
reason why poetry is sometimes difficult to identify. Another is that
several formal features that we associate with poetry are not
discernible in ancient Near Eastern poetry in general and
biblical poetry in particular. For example, rhyme is seldom used,
although assonance and alliteration occasionally are. Moreover,
the meter of biblical poetry is not fully understood. Presumably the
Israelites, and many of their neighbors, used a variety of patterned
rhythms, but there is no consensus about how to analyze them.

The most easily recognizable feature of biblical poetry is known
as parallelism, in which an idea expressed in one line is expressed
in different words in the next. The result is a kind of thought
rhyme. The parallelism may be synonymous, as in:

> Know well the condition of your flocks,
> > and give attention to your herds. (Prov. 27:23)

It may also be contrasting:

> A soft answer turns away wrath,

but a harsh tongue stirs up anger. (Prov. 15:1)

Finally, it may also be progressive:

> As a door turns on its hinges,
>> so does a lazy man in bed. (Prov. 26:14)

Parallel examples of parallelism

As a poetic device parallelism was widely used. In an ancient Canaanite myth, the storm god Baal is told how he will defeat his adversary, Prince Sea:

> Let me tell you, Prince Baal,
>> let me repeat, Rider on the Clouds:
> behold, your enemy, Baal,
>> behold, you will kill your enemy,
>> behold, you will annihilate your foes.
> You will take your eternal kingship,
>> your dominion forever and ever.

In these lines two couplets with synonymous parallelism frame a triplet with both progressive and synonymous parallelism.

Both the techniques and the formulation are familiar to readers of the Bible:

> Behold, your enemies, O Yahweh,
>> behold, your enemies will perish;
>> all evildoers will be scattered. (Ps. 92:9)
> Your kingdom is an eternal kingdom,
>> your rule is forever and ever. (Ps. 145:13)

Further examples are found in many of the poetic passages quoted throughout this book.

Taken on its own, this last proverb may appear to be prose rather than poetry, but because it occurs in a context of proverbs that use parallelism, it too should be considered poetic.

Many variations on these types occur, but the overall pattern is transparent and forms an essential formal element of biblical poetry and of much ancient nonbiblical poetry as well. Given the ongoing use of the Bible in Judaism and Christianity, it is also convenient, to say the least, that unlike rhyme or meter, parallelism is easy to convey in translation.

Poems are scattered throughout the narrative books that form the Torah and the Former Prophets, that is, from Genesis through 2 Kings. We find much more poetry in the Latter Prophets, especially in the books of Isaiah, Jeremiah, and many of the twelve Minor Prophets. There are also books in the Writings that are entirely in poetic form. One is the book of Psalms, the hymnbook of ancient Israel. Another is the relatively short Song of Solomon (also called the Song of Songs), a collection of often erotic love poems between a man and a woman.

Wisdom literature

In ancient Israel as in the rest of the ancient Near East, one kind of writing that frequently employed poetry is what scholars call wisdom literature. The term is broad, including genres such as hymns, disputations, fables, and especially proverbs. Whatever the genre used, wisdom literature focuses on the human condition and is often universal in the sense that it is not linked to particular historical events or individuals. In part because of its universality, wisdom literature was international, with remarkable cross-fertilization among various cultures.

One of the most widely attested genres is the proverb: a pithy saying, often in poetic form, that cleverly expresses a facet of experience. Proverbs are scattered throughout the Bible and also

The international character of wisdom literature is illustrated by the connection between "the words of the wise" in Proverbs 22:17—24:22 and "The Instruction of Amenemope," a late second-millennium BCE Egyptian text. Both are divided into thirty units; among their many parallels are:

Do not make friends with one given to anger,
  and do not visit a man who is hotheaded. (Prov. 22:24)
Do not befriend the heated man,
  nor approach him for conversation. (Amenemope XI.13–14)
Do not move the ancient boundary
  that your fathers made. (Prov. 22:29)
Do not move the markers on the borders of fields
  nor shift the position of the measuring cords. (Amenemope
                                                    VII.12–13)
Do you see a man who is skillful in his work?
  He will be established in the presence of kings. (Prov. 22:29)
The scribe who is skilled in his office,
  he is found worthy to be a courtier. (Amenemope
                                           XXVII.16–17)[1]

clustered in one book, the book of Proverbs. These proverbs most likely began as folk wisdom that scribes collected, expanded, and in some cases at least cast into poetic form. These scribes were often under royal patronage, as editorial notes in the book of Proverbs indicate; for example, "These also are proverbs of Solomon which the men of Hezekiah, king of Judah, collected" (Prov. 25:1). That heading, like a half dozen others found in the book, also illustrates the nature of the book of Proverbs as an anthology of several originally independent collections.

Reflecting this setting in royal courts, some proverbs are a kind of guide to etiquette and advancement, dealing with such issues as table manners in the presence of the king and proper and improper speech. Others treat larger ethical questions—honesty in business, treatment of the needy, respect for parents.

Given the close connection between religious observance and ordinary life in ancient Israel, not surprisingly many of the proverbs also have religious content, stressing that the ultimate path to success is what they call "fear of the LORD," that is, obeying divinely given commands. For the prophets, this has primarily a communal dimension: Yahweh would reward the nation for its obedience and punish it for its rebellion. In Proverbs this same notion of divine justice, or, as it is often called, theodicy, is applied to the individual:

> Honor Yahweh with your wealth
>> and with the first fruits of all your produce;
> then your barns will be filled with plenty,
>> and your vats will be bursting with new wine. (Prov. 3:9–10)
> The reward for humility and fear of Yahweh
>> is riches and honor and long life. (22:4)

Underlying such sentiments is a compelling vision of a powerful deity who is intimately involved in human affairs. That view eventually led to the development of monotheism, the belief that the god of Israel was the only God, who controlled history on all levels, from international relations to ordinary life.

The problem of divine justice

In monotheism, there is only one God, by definition all-good, all-powerful, all-just, rewarding the good and punishing the wicked. But experience shows that this is not always the case—innocent people suffer, wicked people prosper. This profound issue is addressed at length in two biblical books. One is the book of Ecclesiastes, written in a philosophical style in the fourth century BCE. Like Socrates or Diogenes, its anonymous author describes his search for the meaning of life. He observes that contrary to conventional wisdom, the innocent sometimes perish despite their innocence, and the wicked sometimes flourish—God does not, or at least does not seem to, always reward goodness and punish wickedness. What is one to do in the face of this dilemma? The conclusion of Ecclesiastes is almost existential: eat, drink and be

Afterlife in the Old Testament

Because the Old Testament's constituent parts were written over the course of many centuries, it is risky to generalize about the biblical view of almost anything, since on many issues there was development in thinking and also disagreement. This is especially true when we try to determine what the ancient Israelites believed about life after death.

The practice of consulting the dead, necromancy, confirms that there was some notion of survival beyond the grave. Although prohibited, it was widely practiced, and in at least one case was successful, when at King Saul's request a woman who was a medium summoned the dead prophet Samuel from the underworld. But unlike the ancient Egyptians, who were obsessed with life after death, as their elaborate tombs demonstrate, the ancient Israelites give us scant information about it. All the dead lived in a place called Sheol, a dark and dank place, more like the Greek Hades than the blessed west of the Egyptians. There was no contact with God in Sheol, and ordinary life apparently had ended. Ecclesiastes describes it this way: "The dead know nothing . . . There is no work or thought or knowledge or wisdom in Sheol" (Eccles. 9:5, 10). Only relatively late in the biblical period, partly in an effort to resolve the problem of inconsistent divine justice in this life, did Jews begin to develop a more elaborate set of beliefs about the afterlife as a place of reward for the just and punishment for the wicked. This would eventually become the familiar heaven and hell, which Christians and Muslims adopted.

merry, enjoy life as long as you have it, because we all die, and that is the end.

The book of Job

A fuller examination of the problem of theodicy than that of Ecclesiastes is the book of Job. It is one of the most difficult books of the Bible, not only because of its frequently obscure language and somewhat flawed structure, but mostly because of the questions it asks and leaves unanswered.

The framework of the book is prose, and it reads like a reworked ancient folktale. In the prologue, chapters 1 and 2, we are introduced to Job as a perfect man, who "feared God and turned away from evil" (1:1). His piety had been rewarded by great wealth and a large family—seven sons and three daughters. One day, at a meeting of the divine council, Yahweh engaged in a debate with a mysterious figure called the *satan* over whether Job's piety was authentic—was he a God-fearer because it was to his advantage? What if he were stripped of his wealth? Job, the quintessentially innocent, has become the stakes in a cosmic wager.

With divine approval, the *satan* apparently causes a series of disasters, in which Job's many herds of animals were captured or killed, and finally, most horribly, his ten children were killed as well. Job's response, later to be characterized as "the patience of Job" (James 5:11), shows that his piety is authentic: "Yahweh has given; Yahweh has taken away. Blessed be the name of Yahweh" (Job 1:21). At the next meeting of the council, Yahweh confronts the *satan* again: Job "still persists in his integrity, although you incited me against him without cause" (Job 2:3). The *satan* retorts that the true test will be Job's own person, and, again with divine approval, he afflicts Job with a skin disease. Job sits among the ashes, scratching himself with a broken piece of pottery, but does not "sin with his lips" (2:10).

The *satan* is apparently one of the "sons of God," a member of the divine council. His title means "accuser"—perhaps even, in the forensic language that permeates the book, something like a prosecutor. This figure will later become Satan, the devil of Jewish and Christian tradition, but he is not that yet. He is only a kind of foil, who disappears from the book after chapter 2—both Job's friends and Job himself attribute his suffering directly to God.

The narrative prologue sets the stage for an extended discussion of the problem of divine justice in chapters 3–41, cast as a series of dialogues between Job and three of his friends, and finally between Job and Yahweh himself. There are many critical problems with the dialogues, and they seem to be in some disarray, especially in chapters 24–28. The book has also undergone considerable revision, as the unexpected appearance of a fourth friend in chapters 32-37 shows. But the core of the dialogues is a sustained consideration of Job's case. His three friends proclaim the traditional view: God is just, and thus Job is suffering because he must have done something wrong; his children died because they too must have sinned.

Job angrily rejects these platitudes, insisting on his innocence—a claim that we the readers know to be true—and that he had lived up to the highest ideals of Israelites:

> I delivered the poor who cried,
>> and the orphan who had no helper.
> The blessing of the wretched came upon me,
>> and I caused the widow's heart to sing for joy...
> I was eyes to the blind,
>> and feet to the lame.
> I was a father to the needy,
>> and I championed the cause of those I knew not. (Job 29:13–16)

Finally, using another legal metaphor, Job issues God a subpoena: "Here is my signature—let the Almighty answer me!" (31:35).

Then Yahweh does answer Job, appearing to him from the tempest. The divine answer is a series of rhetorical questions to Job, mocking his claim to wisdom:

> Where were you when I laid the foundation of the earth?
>> Tell me, if you have understanding.
> Who determined its measurements—surely you know!
>> Or who stretched the line upon it?
> On what were its bases sunk,
>> or who laid its cornerstone
> when the morning stars sang together
>> and all the sons of God shouted for joy? (Job 38:4–7)

For three chapters (Job 38–41), the divine architect rants on. He describes his power—how he set limits for the proud waves of the sea and made the primeval monster Leviathan his pet—and catalogues the wonders of the natural order. These divine speeches contain some of the most magnificent poetry in the Bible, yet they completely ignore Job's complaint.

Job replies, in words whose Hebrew is difficult and whose meaning is debated; here is a relatively free translation, in which the italicized parts are quotations from God's earlier speeches:

> I know that you can do all things
>> and nothing you wish is impossible.
> *Who is this whose ignorant words*
>> *cover my design with darkness?*
> I have spoken of the unspeakable,
>> and tried to grasp the infinite.
> *Listen, and I will speak;*
>> *I will question you; please, instruct me.*
> I had heard of you with my ears;
>> but now my eyes have seen you.
> Therefore I will be quiet,
>> comforted that I am dust. (Job 42:1–6)[2]

What do these final words of Job mean? That having seen God, his consciousness had been raised, and he knows that there are limits to human wisdom? If so, Job is apparently satisfied. But are we? Some modern readers have interpreted Job's words to mean that Job realizes that his situation is hopeless and is saying anything, anything, to get this blustering tyrant to shut up; an alternative, even freer translation of the last verse is "I shudder with sorrow for mortal clay."[3]

In the prose epilogue (Job 42:7–17) we are returned to the ancient folktale. Yahweh rebukes Job's friends, for they have not spoken the truth as Job did. Then Yahweh restores Job's fortunes, doubling the property that had been lost. Is this an implicit admission of divine culpability? In biblical law such punitive damages are prescribed in cases of theft (Exod. 22:4–9). Finally, Job has more children, again seven sons and three daughters, to replace those who had been killed, and like the patriarchs of old, he dies at a ripe old age. It is, one might think, a happy ending. But again, we may pose a question—what of the dead children, who lost their lives to prove Yahweh's point?

Illustrating the universality of wisdom literature, it is significant that Job himself is not an Israelite—he lives in Uz, somewhere in Edom outside the Promised Land. Although the anonymous author of the book is an Israelite—the book itself is permeated by quotations from and allusions to other biblical texts—in the dialogues Job and his friends do not call God "Yahweh"—only the narrator does. Moreover, the book is remarkable for its lack of explicit reference to the main events and personalities of the Bible: there is no mention of Abraham, Moses, or David, nor of Sinai or Jerusalem. The deity who reveals himself to Job is not the lord of history but a god of nature. These silences suggest one possible interpretation of this challenging book: history, whether of an individual or of a people, is opaque: it does not reveal the actions of a just God who rewards goodness and punishes wickedness.

Other interpretations are also possible, and not necessarily mutually exclusive. Perhaps because of his experience of the transcendent creator, Job has become like the mystics of many religions, surrendering himself in faith to a reality greater than himself in whose presence his own concerns fade into insignificance. Or the ambiguity of Job's final speech and the book's many unanswered questions may be deliberate: perhaps the questions are more important than any formulaic answer.

In its attack on the dominant biblical view of theodicy, the book of Job illustrates yet again that the Bible speaks not with one voice but with many, and that the presence of those differing perspectives invites, even compels, readers to think for themselves.

Chapter 11
"Let us now praise famous men"—and women

The quotation in the chapter title is the opening phrase of a lengthy poetic summary of major and minor characters of biblical literature, written in the early second century BCE by the Jewish author known as Ben Sira, or Sirach, and preserved in the book that bears his name (also known as Ecclesiasticus), one of the Apocrypha in the Christian canon. For six chapters (beginning in 44:1), Ben Sira gives readers an overview of those "whose name lives on and on," including Enoch and Noah in the opening chapters of Genesis, Israel's ancestors Abraham, Isaac, and Jacob, notable leaders and prophets such as Moses, Aaron, Joshua, Samuel, David, Solomon, Elijah, Elisha, Hezekiah, Josiah, Ezekiel, and other remarkable characters found in the pages of the Bible. Three of these characters illustrate the ongoing importance of the Bible, as well as issues concerning its interpretation.

Abraham

Abraham, says Ben Sira, was "the great father of a multitude of nations" (Sir. 44:19, quoting Gen. 17:4), with whom God made a covenant to multiply his descendants and to give them an inheritance—the Promised Land. Abraham is the principal character in Genesis 12–25, along with his wives Sarah and Hagar, his sons Ishmael and Isaac, and his nephew Lot. His story begins abruptly, as with no apparent motivation Yahweh summons him to leave his homeland and to move to a new land, the land of Canaan. There God repeatedly appears to him reaffirming his promise.

There is a mythical dimension to the narratives about Abraham. He often speaks directly with Yahweh, and on one occasion Yahweh even visits him for a meal. But was there ever an Abraham? Or is he just a legendary ancestor, like Romulus, the supposed founder of Rome? We cannot say. Not surprisingly, there are no contemporaneous nonbiblical sources corroborating either the individuals or the events described in Genesis. Because Genesis depicts Abraham, Isaac, and Jacob as semi-nomadic pastoralists wandering with their flocks on the fringes of the larger urban centers of their days, they were at most extras on the larger stage of their times. They would not have invited enough attention to require mention in official records, of which we have only a few from the land of Canaan during most of the second millennium BCE. Moreover, the biblical narrative is complex and multilayered, originating many centuries after any time that Abraham could plausibly have lived. A few clues hint that beneath the sources used by the biblical writers there is some historical memory, but they are subtle clues at best.

We should probably be content to take Abraham as an idealized ancestor: Abraham "believed in Yahweh, and Yahweh considered him righteous" (Gen. 15:6). He always complied with divine commands—emigration, circumcision, even the sacrifice of his son Isaac. As the nineteenth-century Danish philosopher Søren Kierkegaard aptly called him, Abraham was a "knight of faith." On occasion he could challenge Yahweh to act justly, not to let the innocent in Sodom perish while he punished the guilty—the very issue raised in the book of Job. In this too he is something of a model, anticipating Moses, Job, Jeremiah, and other biblical characters who argued with God.

The narrative about Abraham also serves as a kind of overture to the books of the Bible that follow. He is the ancestor of a nation covenanted with God, one given, or at least promised, a land of its own. The relationship of that nation with its Promised Land—the "holy land" (Zech. 2:12) is a central biblical theme, and one that reverberates throughout subsequent Jewish history, whether Abraham's descendants are in the land or exiled from it.

At the same time, as modern or even postmodern readers, we cannot help but observe that sometimes Abraham is less than a paragon. He was capable of deception: when he entered Egypt he told his wife Sarah to say that she was his sister, fearing that when the Egyptians saw how beautiful she was they would kill him and

Abraham, Father of Believers

Judaism, Christianity, and Islam are often designated the "Abrahamic" religions because of their genetic and spiritual links with Abraham. Through his son Isaac and his grandson Jacob, Abraham was the ancestor of the Israelites, and thus of the Jewish people.

Jesus of Nazareth was a Jew, and his genealogies link him directly with Abraham. For Christians Abraham also serves as a model of faith, a kind of spiritual ancestor.

Abraham's oldest son was Ishmael, and from him other peoples were descended, including those we now call Arabs, one of whom was the prophet Muhammad, the human founder of Islam. Thus, like Christianity, Islam has a genealogical link with Abraham, and for Muslims, too, Abraham is a model, especially in his surrender to God (for that is what "Islam" means).

Abraham's importance for all three religions is also clear in their scriptures. He is mentioned more than five dozen times each in the Old Testament after the narrative of his death in Genesis 25, in the New Testament, and in the Qur'an.

take her. Sarah did so, and thus became part of Pharaoh's harem, but Abraham's life was spared. Our discomfort at this selfish duplicity is not necessarily anachronistic sensitivity to women's equality: the same story has a variant in Genesis in which Abraham does not lie, because Sarah, the narrator incredibly tells us, was Abraham's half-sister. Abraham's willingness to sacrifice Isaac as God ordered, although praised since antiquity, is even more troubling: why would he *not* question such a horrific divine command? After all, he had boldly urged God to spare the lives of the innocent citizens of Sodom—why did he not plead for Isaac? Questions such as these arise from the complexity of the text itself, which thus invites interpretation by readers.

Deborah

Ben Sira's catalogue includes only men—he was something of a male chauvinist, if not a misogynist. But the pages of the Bible include not just the stories of men: from the opening chapters of Genesis on we are introduced to remarkable female characters— independent women, strong women, women who deal directly with God and lead their people. To be sure, some of the women of the Bible are unnamed, such as Noah's wife, Pharaoh's daughter, and Job's wife, probably because the patriarchalism of ancient biblical writers saw them only as adjuncts of their male protectors. But well over one hundred women are named, including the matriarchs Sarah, Hagar, Rebekah, Leah, Rachel, Zilpah, and Bilhah; the prophets Miriam, Huldah, and Noadiah; and queens and queen mothers, such as Bathsheba, Jezebel, and Athaliah.

Deborah is one of these named women, whom we may take as representative of them all. She is the principal character of a brief episode in the book of Judges, which is set in the transitional period between the death of Joshua, who had led the Israelites into the Promised Land after Moses's death, and the beginning of monarchy under Saul, as related in 1 Samuel. The book is named for the twelve individuals called "judges," a term that in ancient

Israel as elsewhere in the ancient Near East designates leaders who exercised not only judicial but also military and political functions. Eleven of the twelve judges in the book are men; the exception is Deborah, who is also identified as a prophet.

There are two overlapping accounts of her activity, a prose narrative in Judges 4, and a very old poem in Judges 5, the "Song of Deborah." According to Judges 4, as she sat in judgment under a palm tree Deborah sent for Barak and instructed him to muster troops from the tribes of Naphtali and Zebulun and to join her in an attack on the Canaanites, who were oppressing the Israelites. In this shared leadership, Deborah takes the initiative and also decides on the strategy to defeat the Canaanites. In the aftermath of the battle, the fleeing general of the Canaanites was killed by another woman, Jael.

Following the prose narrative is a poem celebrating the victory, according to its heading sung by Deborah and Barak. This poem, one of the oldest in the Bible, describes how Yahweh fought alongside his people; like the prose text that precedes it and is probably derived from it, the poem mentions Deborah and Barak together as military leaders in the victory.

Because of her active military role, Deborah differs from women such as Rahab, Jael, and Delilah, who aided their allies but not as warriors. In later Jewish and Christian sources Deborah becomes the prototype of the warrior woman: both Judith in the book of the Apocrypha named for her and Joan of Arc are modeled on Deborah.

We know little more of Deborah. She is called "the wife of Lappidoth" (Judg. 4:4) and so apparently was married, although the phrase thus translated can also mean "woman of torches" and could refer to her incendiary character; perhaps not coincidentally, Barak's name means "lightning." She was "a mother in Israel" (Judg. 5:7), but what that means is unclear: Was she the leader of a prophetic group, whose leader if male would be its "father"? Or was she an authority figure, who if male could be a "father"? Or was she actually a mother with children? If so, the poem may imply amazement at how she transcended the typical status of a wife and mother.

The figure of Deborah raises again the complicated issue of the status of women in ancient Israel. Were her activities as prophet, judge, and warrior exceptional? Perhaps—that the Canaanite general Sisera was killed by a woman was apparently especially shameful. Yet apart from that hint, the biblical writers express no surprise at what Deborah accomplished, and we must be careful not to overstate the subordination of women to men in biblical times. In any case, we are fortunate to have this glimpse of a powerful woman, leading Israelite volunteer militia into battle.

David

David, the second king of Israel and the founder of a dynasty that lasted more than four centuries, pervades biblical tradition, with more space devoted to him and to compositions attributed to him than to any other human character in the Hebrew Bible except for Moses. As is also true of Moses, we have no independent confirmation that David ever existed, but all except the most skeptical scholars think that the broad outlines of his life as presented in the Bible are historically accurate.

The primary narrative of David's rise from shepherd to king of Israel and of his long reign is 1 Samuel 16–1 Kings 2. Like other extended narratives in the Bible, it is very much a composite. Drawing on a variety of sources, the biblical historians construct a picture of a complex character—as the subtitle of a recent book about David aptly puts it, he was "messiah, murderer, traitor, king."[1]

His capsule biography is as follows. Born in Bethlehem as the youngest of seven brothers, he was unlikely to get any substantial inheritance, and so he joined the newly formed army of Israel's first king, Saul. In it he excelled as a warrior, and he married Saul's daughter Michal. Eventually, however, he and Saul had a falling out, and David and men personally loyal to him became mercenaries for Israel's enemies, the Philistines. Near the end of the eleventh century BCE, when Saul died in battle against the Philistines, David became king, first of the southern tribe of Judah and then of the northern tribes, uniting the kingdom under himself in his newly designated capital, Jerusalem. He reportedly ruled for some forty years, perhaps a formulaic round number, but in any case a long reign. During it he was able to dominate the larger region, in part because of the relative weakness of the great powers of Egypt and Mesopotamia. After some murderous rivalry among his sons, he named one of them, Solomon, as his successor before he died.

In the primary narrative about David we are given a multidimensional portrait of a gifted, even charismatic leader. David was a brilliant military strategist, as legends about his early prowess as well as his victories as king show. He was a consummate politician, rapidly achieving prominence in Saul's court, and able to persuade both northern and southern Israelites to accept him as king even though he had fought for the Philistines. He was also a talented poet and musician. Several poems attributed to David are included in 2 Samuel, and one that is almost certainly authentic is his lament for Saul and Saul's son Jonathan, David's close friend (2 Sam. 1:17–27). Because of David's reputation as composer and lyricist, authorship of many other biblical poems, including half of the Psalms, was attributed to this "sweet singer of Israel" (2 Sam. 23:1).

This sketch is based on various types of evidence, much of it propaganda. But not all. There was another side to David, which the biblical historians also present in detail. The opening words of

Jerusalem, the holy city

According to 2 Samuel 5, toward the beginning of his reign David moved his capital from Hebron, the traditional site of the burial of Abraham and his family, to the non-Israelite city of Jerusalem, which became known as the city of David. Then, to provide divine legitimation for his rule, he brought the ark of the covenant to Jerusalem, so that the city of David also became the city of God.

David's son Solomon built the First Temple there, so Jerusalem became the religious center of ancient Israel and thus the geographical focus of Judaism. The prayer "Next year in Jerusalem" near the conclusion of the Passover seder illustrates this centrality, as does the late biblical identification of the site of the Temple as the mountain where Abraham was to sacrifice Isaac (2 Chron. 3:1).

As an observant Jew, Jesus went to Jerusalem to celebrate the Passover, and there, the Gospels tell us, he was arrested, executed, buried, and, according to Christian belief, raised from the dead. Because these events took place in Jerusalem, it became the holy city for Christians.

Muslims accept as essentially valid the earlier revelations found in the Bible, and so for them Jerusalem is also sacred because of its associations with David, Solomon, and Jesus. Jerusalem's status for Muslims is further enhanced because according to Muslim legend, the prophet Muhammad himself was miraculously transported from Mecca to Jerusalem, from which he was taken to heaven to converse with God.

Jerusalem's continuing importance as holy city for Jews, Christians, and Muslims—and hence as focus of conflict in the Middle East—is directly due to David's having made it his capital more than three thousand years ago.

the account of his affair with Bathsheba are: "Now it was the springtime, the time when kings go forth to war, but David stayed in Jerusalem" (2 Sam. 11:1). David's army, along with the ark of the covenant, was across the Jordan in Ammon, attacking its capital Rabbah. True kings, the narrator implies, are with their troops— but not David. And because he stayed in Jerusalem, he glimpsed Bathsheba bathing, slept with her, and then recalled her husband Uriah from the battlefield so that the pregnancy that had resulted would be attributed to him. When Uriah refused the comforts of home, David sent him back with sealed instructions that he be stationed in a vulnerable part of the battlefield and left undefended. So David, the warrior, the king, the poet, was also an adulterer and a murderer by proxy, and he is rebuked by the prophet Nathan for his actions. The biblical writers tell us all this and much more, depicting David as a deeply flawed hero.

Despite the very mixed view we get of David from the primary narrative, subsequent literature glossed over the reprehensible aspects of his life. For the authors of the book of Kings he became the model king, the touchstone against whom all subsequent rulers of his dynasty were assessed, usually negatively. When the authors of the books of Chronicles, writing in the fifth or fourth century BCE, retold the story of David, although they used the books of Samuel as their principal source, they omitted any negative aspects, such as the Bathsheba affair and his son Absalom's revolt. Finally, because his reign was remembered as a time of peace and prosperity, and therefore one of special divine blessing, later generations would model a hoped-for future leader on this "anointed of the god of Jacob" (2 Sam. 23:1).

An anonymous early Christian writer wrote a catalogue of Israelite heroes similar to that of Ben Sira and concluded with a summary of the "cloud of witnesses" too numerous to mention:

> And what more should I say? For time would fail me to tell of
> Gideon, Barak, Samson, Jephthah, of David and Samuel and the

prophets—who through faith conquered kingdoms, administered justice, obtained promises, shut the mouths of lions, quenched raging fire, escaped the edge of the sword, won strength out of weakness, became mighty in war, put foreign armies to flight. (Heb. 11:32–34)

For this author, as for Ben Sira, these individuals are heroic models, and believers have continued to view them as such. Many are also engaging literary characters, whose narratives have fascinated readers and inspired writers, artists, and composers regardless of their own beliefs.

Chapter 12
The enduring significance of the Old Testament

Museum visitors may be tourists, intending to broaden and deepen their appreciation of culture. For the last two millennia, the Bible has been an inspiration to creative artists—sculptors, painters, playwrights, novelists, composers, choreographers, and many others. They have taken biblical personalities and events and interpreted them in their respective media. This influence of the Bible is so pervasive that to make a catalogue of artistic works based on the Bible would be not just tedious but virtually impossible. To take just one example, there are thematic allusions to the book of Job in the works of Melville, Dostoyevsky, Kafka, and Beckett, and in the twentieth century alone more than a dozen novels and plays based on it by such writers as H. G. Wells, Muriel Spark, Neil Simon, Robert Frost, Robert Heinlein, and Archibald MacLeish. A recent *catalogue raisonnée* of the book of Job in art contains some 150 examples of artists' interpretations of the book of Job from the third century CE through the twentieth.

The Bible has also repeatedly been used in popular culture—in films, songs, and musical comedies (there is even one based on the book of Job). Biblical phrases permeate casual speech, often in clichés whose origin may be unrecognized, such as "the skin of my teeth," taken from Job 19:20. And, for better and for worse, the Bible has influenced such fields as law, medicine, science, and politics.

To appreciate these myriad cultural connections, it is not necessary either to be familiar with the biblical traditions or to be a believer, just as Bach's cantatas with biblical librettos can be heard in a concert hall as well as in a church. Moreover, just as Brahms's *German Requiem* was written for concert performance rather than for a funeral, and Bernstein's *Mass* was intended for the stage, so too the Bible continues to be used by creative artists without necessarily explicit religious intent. Because biblical characters, events, and ideals are woven into the fabric of our culture, knowing them helps us better understand our past and therefore ourselves.

Museum visitors may also be pilgrims, in a sense. For Jews and for Christians, despite some differences in content and order, the Hebrew Bible, the Old Testament, is sacred scripture and as such has a special authority. Its significance is axiomatic and needs no rationale. For believers it is heard and read as Monteverdi's masses and Bach's cantatas were in their original liturgical settings, in the context of a community of believers.

For individuals and communities of faith throughout the ages, the Bible in all its complexity has been understood as a single book, written by a single divine author. Yet many voices are preserved in the Old Testament, and a crucial issue of interpretation is how to hear those voices. Should we, as modern critical scholars have suggested, try to distinguish them, in their particularity, paying attention to what each voice is saying? Or should we, as premodern and some postmodern scholars have suggested, focus on the polyphonous effect of the whole? Perhaps both are necessary and possible.

Consider the notion of generational punishment. The Ten Commandments state it explicitly:

> I the LORD your God am a jealous God, punishing sons for the iniquity of fathers, to the third and the fourth generation of those who hate me, but showing steadfast love to the thousandth

generation of those who love me and keep my commandments.
(Exod. 20:5–6)

Yet this understanding of divinely imposed collective punishment is elsewhere explicitly contradicted, as by the prophet Ezekiel:

> The person who sins shall die. A son shall not suffer for the iniquity
> of a father, nor a father suffer for the iniquity of a son; the
> righteousness of the righteous shall be his own, and the wickedness
> of the wicked shall be his own. (Ezek. 18:20)

For the prophet, divine justice should correspond to a principle of the Israelite legal system, according to which "fathers shall not be put to death for their sons, nor shall sons be put to death for their parents; only for his own crime may a man be put to death" (Deut. 24:16). In Ezekiel, then, we have a development in thinking, even an outright rejection of an earlier view enshrined in the Decalogue and attributed to God himself.

As this example shows, the multiplicity of voices in the Old Testament requires that readers engage in interpretation, since the different voices are not always in harmony. Moreover, because of this often dissonant polyphony, any argument based solely on what the Bible says, as though it speaks with only one voice, is fundamentally flawed. As Shakespeare observed, even "the Devil can cite Scripture for his purpose" (*Merchant of Venice* I.iii), and politicians, pundits, and popes who use it as a collection of proof texts to be selected almost at random, disregarding original meaning and context, do so by ignoring the book as a whole. Moreover, no community of faith today would accept every biblical command as binding, so the view of the Bible as an absolute and timeless authority is challenged both within the Bible itself and in subsequent religious history.

The relationship between an authoritative scripture and the community that considers it such is complex. The text shapes the community—its beliefs, its values, and its practices. At the same time, the community in a very real way shapes the text as well. The text is not, except perhaps in the abstract, intrinsically authoritative: it derives its authority from the community. And that community—or rather, in the case of the Bible, those interrelated communities—has a continuous history which cumulatively provides authority both to the text and to the processes of expansion, modification, interpretation, reinterpretation, adaptation, and even selective rejection of biblical traditions. The processes are ongoing, as ancient texts are continually accommodated to suit new circumstances, and what these texts meant becomes intertwined with what they mean. The many voices heard in the pages of the Bible, themselves coming from different times and contexts, begin these multiple processes, and so the processes are first authorized by the Bible itself.

Reading the Bible, then, is difficult, but it is also rewarding. Its many voices unite in celebrating Yahweh, the god of Israel, a god passionately if mysteriously engaged with the world and the humans who inhabit it.

Chronology

Date*	Events and persons	Biblical books**
Early–mid-second millennium (?)	Ancestors of Israel: Abraham, Isaac, Jacob	*Genesis*
Thirteenth century (?)	Exodus from Egypt: Moses	*Exodus– Deuteronomy*
Late second millennium	Emergence of Israel in the land of Canaan	*Joshua; Judges*
Late eleventh–late tenth centuries	Establishment of the monarchy: Samuel, Saul, David, Solomon	*1-2 Samuel; 1 Kings 1-11*
Late tenth–mid-eighth centuries	Divided monarchies of Israel and Judah	*1 Kings 12- 2 Kings 14*
Mid-ninth–mid-seventh centuries	Assyrian control of Near East	*2 Kings 15-23;* Amos; Hosea
722	Assyrians defeat Northern Kingdom of Israel and destroy Samaria, its capital	*2 Kings 17;* Isaiah 1-12; Micah
701	Assyrians attack Southern Kingdom of Judah and lay siege to Jerusalem, its capital, but do not destroy it	*2 Kings 18-20 (=Isaiah 36- 37);* Isaiah 1:7-9; 10:5-11

(Continued)

Date*	Events and persons	Biblical books**
622	Reform of King Josiah of Judah	*2 Kings 22–23*
Late seventh–mid-sixth centuries	Babylonian control of Near East	
597	First siege of Jerusalem by the Babylonian king Nebuchadrezzar	*2 Kings 24:10–17*
586	Destruction of Jerusalem by Nebuchadrezzar and Babylonian exile	*2 Kings 25*; Jeremiah; Ezekiel
Mid-sixth–late fourth centuries	Persian control of Near East	*Ezra–Nehemiah*
538	Return of some exiles to Judah	
Late fourth–early first centuries	Greek control of Near East	Sirach; Daniel
168	Revolt of the Maccabees	*1–2 Maccabees*
63	Roman general Pompey captures Jerusalem	

*All dates are BCE. A question mark indicates that the date is disputed, or there is insufficient evidence.

**Italics indicate the narrative chronology of the book; normal font indicates the book's primary date of composition.

Appendix

The Canons of the Hebrew Bible/Old Testament

JUDAISM	CHRISTIANITY		
Hebrew Bible (Tanak)	*Old Testament*		
	PROTESTANT	ROMAN CATHOLIC	EASTERN ORTHODOX
Torah	**[Pentateuch]**		
Genesis	Genesis	Genesis	Genesis
Exodus	Exodus	Exodus	Exodus
Leviticus	Leviticus	Leviticus	Leviticus
Numbers	Numbers	Numbers	Numbers
Deuteronomy	Deuteronomy	Deuteronomy	Deuteronomy
Prophets (Neviim)			
FORMER PROPHETS	**[Historical Books]**		
Joshua	Joshua	Joshua	Joshua
Judges	Judges	Judges	Judges
1 & 2 Samuel	Ruth	Ruth	Ruth
1 & 2 Kings	1 & 2 Samuel	1 & 2 Samuel	1 & 2 Samuel
LATTER PROPHETS	1 & 2 Kings	1 & 2 Kings	1 & 2 Kings
Isaiah	1 & 2 Chronicles	1 & 2 Chronicles	1 & 2 Chronicles

(Continued)

Hebrew Bible (Tanak)	*Old Testament*		
		ROMAN	EASTERN
	PROTESTANT	CATHOLIC	ORTHODOX
Jeremiah	Ezra	Ezra	Ezra
Ezekiel	Nehemiah	Nehemiah	1 Esdras
The Twelve	Esther	Tobit	2 Esdras
Hosea		Judith	Nehemiah
Joel		Esther	Tobit
Amos		1 Maccabees	Judith
Obadiah		2 Maccabees	Esther
Jonah			1 Maccabees
Micah			2 Maccabees
Nahum			3 Maccabees
Habakkuk	**[Poetical**		
Zephaniah	**Books]**		
Haggai	Job	Job	Job
Zechariah	Psalms	Psalms	Psalms
Malachi			Psalm 151
			Prayer of
			Manasseh
Writings	Proverbs	Proverbs	Proverbs
(Ketuvim)	Ecclesiastes	Ecclesiastes	Ecclesiastes
Psalms	Song of	Song of	Song of
Proverbs	Solomon	Solomon	Solomon
		Wisdom of	Wisdom of
Job		Solomon	Solomon
		Sirach	Sirach
Five Scrolls		(Ecclesiasticus)	(Ecclesiasticus)
Song of Solomon	**[Prophets]**		
Ruth	Isaiah	Isaiah	Isaiah
Lamentations	Jeremiah	Jeremiah	Jeremiah
Ecclesiastes	Lamentations	Lamentations	Lamentations
Esther		Baruch	Baruch
Daniel			Letter of
			Jeremiah
Ezra-	Ezekiel	Ezekiel	Ezekiel
Nehemiah	Daniel	Daniel	Daniel
1 & 2		Additions to	Additions to
Chronicles		Daniel	Daniel

Hosea	Hosea	Hosea
Joel	Joel	Joel
Amos	Amos	Amos
Obadiah	Obadiah	Obadiah
Jonah	Jonah	Jonah
Micah	Micah	Micah
Nahum	Nahum	Nahum
Habakkuk	Habakkuk	Habakkuk
Zephaniah	Zephaniah	Zephaniah
Haggai	Haggai	Haggai
Zechariah	Zechariah	Zechariah
Malachi	Malachi	Malachi
		(4 Maccabees)

References

Translations from the Bible are usually from the New Revised Standard Version; in some cases I have modified the translation to reflect the meaning of the original more closely. Chapter and verse numbers follow the New Revised Standard Version. Unless credited, translations of other texts are my own.

Chapter 4

1. Stephanie Dalley, *Myths from Mesopotamia* (Oxford: Oxford University Press, 1989), 253.
2. Ibid., 114.

Chapter 6

1. Code of Hammurapi 195, translation adapted from Martha Roth, *Law Collections from Mesopotamia and Asia Minor,* 2nd ed. (Atlanta: Scholars Press, 1997), 120.

Chapter 8

1. Martti Nissinen, *Prophets and Prophecy in the Ancient Near East* (Atlanta: Society of Biblical Literature, 2003), 19–20.

Chapter 9

1. Mordechai Cogan and Hayim Tadmor, *II Kings: A New Translation with Introduction and Commentary,* Anchor Bible 11 (Garden City, NY: Doubleday, 1988), 338–39.

Chapter 10

1. Miriam Lichtheim, *Ancient Egyptian Literature,* vol. 2, *The New Kingdom* (Berkeley: University of California Press, 2006 [1976]), 153, 151, 162.
2. Stephen Mitchell, *The Book of Job* (San Francisco: North Point Press, 1987), 88.
3. Jack Miles, *God: A Biography* (New York: Knopf, 1995), 325.

Chapter 11

1. The subtitle of Baruch Halpern, *David's Secret Demons* (Grand Rapids, MI: Eerdmans, 2001).

Further Reading

Annotated Bibles

Attridge, Harold W., ed. *The HarperCollins Study Bible*. Rev. ed. San Francisco: HarperSanFrancisco, 2006.

Berlin, Adele, and Marc Zvi Brettler, eds. *The Jewish Study Bible*. New York: Oxford University Press, 2004.

Coogan, Michael D., ed. *The New Oxford Annotated Bible with the Apocrypha*. 3rd augmented ed., New York: Oxford University Press, 2007.

Harrelson, Walter J., ed. *The New Interpreter's Study Bible*. Nashville: Abingdon, 2003.

O'Day, Gail R., and David Petersen, eds. *The Access Bible*. New York: Oxford University Press, 1999.

Senior, Donald, and John J. Collins, eds. *The Catholic Study Bible*. 2nd ed. New York: Oxford University Press, 2006.

Introductions

Brettler, Marc Zvi. *How to Read the Jewish Bible*. New York: Oxford University Press, 2007.

Kugel, James L. *How to Read the Bible: A Guide to Scripture Then and Now*. New York: Free Press, 2007.

McKenzie, Steven L. *How to Read the Bible: History, Prophecy, Literature—Why Modern Readers Need to Know the Difference, and What It Means for Faith Today*. New York: Oxford University Press, 2005.

Reference

Achtemeier, Paul J., ed. *The HarperCollins Bible Dictionary.* San Francisco: HarperSanFrancisco, 1996.

Barton, John, and John Muddiman, eds. *The Oxford Bible Commentary.* Oxford: Oxford University Press, 2001.

Freedman, David Noel, ed. *The Anchor Bible Dictionary.* New York: Doubleday, 1992.

Hayes, John H., ed. *Dictionary of Biblical Interpretation.* Nashville: Abingdon, 1999.

Keck, Leander E. et al., eds. *The New Interpreter's Bible.* Nashville: Abingdon, 1994–2004.

Mays, James L., ed. *The HarperCollins Bible Commentary.* San Francisco: HarperSanFrancisco, 2000.

Metzger, Bruce M., and Michael D. Coogan, eds. *The Oxford Companion to the Bible.* New York: Oxford University Press, 1993.

Meyers, Carol, ed. *Women in Scripture: A Dictionary of Named and Unnamed Women in the Hebrew Bible, the Apocryphal/ Deuterocanonical Books, and the New Testament.* Boston: Houghton Mifflin, 2000.

Rogerson, J. W., and Judith M. Lieu, eds. *The Oxford Handbook of Biblical Studies.* Oxford: Oxford University Press, 2006.

Sakenfeld, Katharine Doob, ed. *The New Interpreter's Dictionary of the Bible.* Nashville: Abingdon, 2006–.

van der Toorn, Karel et al., eds. *Dictionary of Deities and Demons in the Bible.* 2nd ed. Leiden: Brill, 1999.

Ancient Near Eastern Texts

Chavalas, Mark W., ed. *The Ancient Near East: Historical Sources in Translation.* Malden, MA: Blackwell, 2006.

Hallo, William W., ed. *The Context of Scripture.* Leiden: Brill, 1997–2002.

Society of Biblical Literature. *Writings from the Ancient World.* Atlanta: Society of Biblical Literature, 1990–.

Canon

Trebolle, Julio. "Canon of the Old Testament." In *The New Interpreter's Dictionary of the Bible,* edited by Katharine Doob Sakenfeld, 1:548–63. Nashville: Abingdon, 2006.

History and Archaeology

Coogan, Michael D., ed. *The Oxford History of the Biblical World*. New York: Oxford University Press, 1998.

King, Philip J., and Lawrence E. Stager. *Life in Biblical Israel*. Louisville: Westminster John Knox, 2001.

Laughlin, John C. H. *Archaeology and the Bible*. London: Routledge, 2000.

Miller, J. Maxwell, and John H. Hayes. *A History of Ancient Israel and Judah*. 2nd ed. Louisville: Westminster John Knox, 2006.

Biblical Religion

Miller, Patrick D. *The Religion of Ancient Israel*. Louisville: Westminster John Knox, 2000.

Smith, Mark S. *The Early History of God: Yahweh and the Other Deities in Ancient Israel*. 2nd ed. Grand Rapids, MI: Eerdmans, 2002.

Prophets

Petersen, David L. *The Prophetic Literature: An Introduction*. Louisville: Westminster John Knox, 2002.

Sweeney, Marvin A. *The Prophetic Literature*. Nashville: Abingdon, 2005.

Job

Newsom, Carol A. *The Book of Job: A Contest of Moral Imaginations*. New York: Oxford University Press, 2003.

Terrien, Samuel L. *The Iconography of Job through the Centuries: Artists as Biblical Interpreters*. University Park: Pennsylvania State University Press, 1996.

Index

Visit the
VERY SHORT
INTRODUCTIONS
Web Sites

www.oup.com/uk/vsi
www.oup.com/us

➤ **Information** about all published titles

➤ News of **forthcoming books**

➤ **Extracts** from the books, including titles not yet published

➤ **Reviews** and views

➤ **Links** to other **web sites** and main OUP web page

➤ Information about **VSIs in translation**

➤ **Contact** the editors

➤ **Order** other **VSIs** on-line

Expand your collection of
VERY SHORT INTRODUCTIONS

THE BIBLE
A Very Short Introduction
John Riches

It is sometimes said that the Bible is one of the most unread books in the
world, yet it has been a major force in the development of Western culture
and continues to exert an enormous influence over many people's lives.
This Very Short Introduction looks at the importance accorded to the Bible
by different communities and cultures and attempts to explain why
it has generated such a rich variety of uses and interpretations. It explores
how the Bible was written, the development of the canon, the role of
Biblical criticism, the appropriation of the Bible in high and popular culture,
and its use for political ends.

"Short in length, but not in substance, nor in interest.
A fascinating introduction both to the way in which the Bible
came to be what it is, and to what it means and has meant for
believers. The examples are well-chosen and involving, and the
discussion is erudite and original."

Joel Marcus, Boston University

www.oup.com/uk/isbn/978-0-19-285343-1

THE DEAD SEA SCROLLS
A Very Short Introduction
Timothy Lim

Since their accidental discovery in 1947, the Dead Sea Scrolls have
been hailed as the greatest manuscript discovery ever. Amidst
conspiracies, politics, and sensational claims, however, it can be difficult
to separate myth from reality.

In this Very Short Introduction, Timothy Lim explores the cultural
and historical background of the scrolls and examines their significance
for our understanding of the Old Testament and the origins of
Christianity and Judaism. He also tells the fascinating story of the
discovery, explains the science of the deciphering and dating, and
does not omit the characters, scandals and controversies that have
elevated the scrolls to the status of cultural icon.

"An excellent addition to the series."

Evangelical Quarterly

www.oup.com/uk/isbn/978-0-19-280659-8

JUDAISM
A Very Short Introduction
Norman Solomon

This Very Short Introduction discusses Judaism as a living religion, in all its contemporary richness and variety. How has it changed since the days of the Bible, or even since the time of Jesus? What sects and divisions does it have, and how does it respond to the challenges of modernity? How does the secular state of Israel resolve the conflicts of "Church" and state?

Norman Solomon provides an accessible and perceptive introduction to the central features and characters of Judaism, from its spiritual leaders, poets, and philosophers, to its eccentrics, including the mystic who tried to convert the pope, and the Berber princess who held up the Arab invasion of Spain.

> "Norman Solomon has achieved the near impossible with his enlightened Very Short Introduction to Judaism. . . . He manages to keep the reader engaged, never patronizes, assumes little knowledge but a keen mind, and takes us through Jewish life and history with such gusto that one feels enlivened, rather than exhausted, at the end."
>
> **Rabbi Julia Neuberger**

www.oup.com/uk/isbn/978-0-19-285390-5

CHRISTIANITY
A Very Short Introduction
Linda Woodhead

This Very Short Introduction offers a candid and wide-ranging overview of the world's largest religion. Linda Woodhead distinguishes three main types of Christianity—Church, Biblical, and Mystical—and examines their struggles with one another and with wider society.

Steering away from an idealistic approach, this introduction considers Christianity's relations with worldly power and its attempts to achieve social, political, economic and cultural dominance. It sheds light on Christianity's changing fortunes, and helps explain why a religion that is currently growing in much of the southern hemisphere is struggling to survive in parts of the West.

"Faced with an almost impossible task of making a coherent and truthful selection of the emphases and themes, I don't think it could have been done better. Though very broad in its range, this is highly informed, observant and wise."

Iain Torrence, President, Princeton Theological Seminary

www.oup.com/uk/isbn/978-0-19-280322-1